What Is Normal Anyway?

What Is Normal Anyway?

The story of an Asperger's Relationship

By Annie Sheridan

Printed by Llanerch Press Ltd 2014

ISBN 978 1 861431 68 4

Acknowledgement

Writing a book, like living a relationship, is not something that can be done alone. Thank you Justine for tireless proof-reading, Lyn for finding me a publisher, and both of you for all the years of friendship, support and patient listening. Thank you Debbie, for enabling me to change manuscript to book, Dave for a cover that does exactly what I wanted and my children just for being there, even though they didn't know what I was doing. Above all, first, last and always, thank you to my wonderful husband, for completing my world and making everything worthwhile.

Annie.

Front cover design by David Michael Higgs.

Foreword

This is an honest, thoughtful and deeply moving account of a difficult but rewarding marriage between an ordinary woman and her husband who has Asperger's syndrome. It will be of tremendous interest not only to couples in similar circumstances but also to anyone - parents, carers, teachers, friends - trying to build and maintain communication with an adult with high-functioning autism or Asperger's syndrome.

After twenty years teaching children on the autistic spectrum I am well-acquainted with the characteristics shown to a greater or lesser extent by all people with autism and Asperger's syndrome. For many of them much of the time the world is a confusing and often frightening place and other people can be very hard to understand and tolerate. All human relationships require work and thought. The marriage so very well described here clearly needs greater than usual commitment on both sides, but hopefully the amount each partner receives will continue to equal the enormous amount of effort each is putting in.

The author reflects on every aspect of daily life with her husband – his obsessions, social interactions, relationships with stepchildren, anxiety, stress and sleep patterns, offering occasional advice clearly based on direct experience. She also discusses their sexual difficulties with openness and sensitivity. She talks about their personal relationship - the honesty, closeness and warmth but the constant need for her to be aware that there are emotional reactions which he cannot understand and finds hard to cope with.

Although the author is often lonely, anxious and frustrated yet she also expresses clearly that this is the marriage she wants and she constantly celebrates her husband's gentleness and honesty and the recurring demonstrations of his love for her. It is a detailed picture and one which must give others in such relationships the support we all find in understanding that our difficulties are shared.

Freja Gregory

(MEd special: Autism)

Bristol   May 2014

Contents

Chapter				Page

Chapter 1

Introduction

"People with Asperger's syndrome perceive the world differently from everyone else. They find the rest of us strange and baffling. Why don't we say what we mean? Why do we say so many things we don't mean? Why do we so often make trivial remarks that mean nothing at all? Why do we get bored and impatient when someone with Asperger's syndrome tells us hundreds of fascinating facts about time-tables, the different varieties of carrots or the movements of the planets? Why do we tolerate such a confusion of sensations of light, sound, smell, touch and taste without getting to screaming pitch? Why do we care about social hierarchies – why not treat everyone in the same way? Why do we have such complicated emotional relationships? Why do we send and receive so many social signals to each other and how do we make sense of them? Above all, why are we all so illogical compared to people with Asperger's syndrome?" Foreword by Lorna Wing in Asperger's Syndrome. A Guide for Parents and Professionals. Tony Attwood.

"What is Asperger's Syndrome? A few years ago hardly anyone had heard of the term, yet today almost every school seems to have a child with this new syndrome. Yet the first definition of such children was first published over 50 years ago by Hans Asperger, a Viennese paediatrician. He identified a consistent pattern of abilities and behaviour that predominantly occurred in boys. The pattern included a lack of empathy, little ability to form friendships, one-sided conversations, intense absorption in a special interest and clumsy movements. However, his pioneering work did not achieve international recognition until the 1990's. Until recently

1

parents and teachers may have realised the child was unusual, but had no idea why, nor knew where to go for help". Asperger's Syndrome. A Guide for Parents and Professionals. Tony Attwood.

The purpose of this book is not to give you scientifically proven facts and figures, gleaned from longitudinal studies of relationships between a 'normal' person and a person with Asperger's syndrome. When I discovered that my new partner, Max, had Asperger's syndrome I knew very little about it, so decided to start researching the condition. It soon became apparent that it is easy to access information about children, but much more difficult to find anything about adults and more specifically relationships between couples where one of them has Asperger's syndrome. This book does not set out to give you any answers to issues you may have within your relationship as every relationship and individual is different. It is a story of our ongoing relationship from its beginnings as a friendship to a romance and marriage. The story is not complete as everyday throws up new challenges, and unexpected twists, but we hope that some of our experiences and the ways we have dealt with them may, in some way, offer the reader the feeling that they are not alone in this struggle. I use this word as it fits perfectly. It is not easy for either partner in this type of relationship as I am sure you have already found out if you have decided to read this book.

Asperger's syndrome is a developmental disorder that people are born with and yet there is a significant stigma attached to it, and a lot of ignorance surrounding it. People associate it with the more aggressive behaviour often associated with the severely Autistic and do not realise there are varying degrees of Autism; Asperger's is considered by many to be at the higher functioning end of the autistic spectrum.

"High-functioning children have great possibilities for compensatory learning. Their intellectual resources allow them to develop alternative means to learn social skills. They may carefully observe the social rules, but still not become integrated into the complex social world." Autism. A very short introduction. Uta Frith 2008.

I have included quotes from several sources in the places I consider relevant as I think it helps understand the context a little better. Max's own words and descriptions have been put in italic's to make it clear that it is his viewpoint and not my interpretation.

Chapter 2

A brief background of Asperger's Syndrome

"Asperger Syndrome is a form of autism and is classified as part of the autism spectrum of disorders, which includes high-functioning autism, and a broader class called 'pervasive developmental disorders' (PDDs) or 'pervasive developmental disorder – not otherwise specified' (PDD – NOS), both very mild forms of autism. It is characterized by difficulty in social interactions and communication, distinctive patterns of behaviour and intense, narrowly focused interests... Asperger syndrome is thought by some to be a form of high functioning autism and the diverse work of both Asperger and Leo Kanner, an Austrian- American psychiatrist, formed the basis of the modern study of autism.....There is debate about the causes of Asperger syndrome, but it may be caused by genetic differences in brain structure, although brain imaging techniques such as functional magnetic resonance imaging (fMRI) scans have not proved conclusively that there is any pathology involved.... The debate continues among clinicians, researchers and people with the condition as to whether it should be called a syndrome, a disorder, or indeed whether it should simply be left as a neurological difference.... It is found at least ten times more commonly in males than females, according to Professor Simon Baron-Cohen of the Autism Research Centre at Cambridge University". Dr Ruth Searle. *Asperger Syndrome in Adults. Sheldon Press 2010.*

I prefer the idea that it is a difference rather than a disorder. We are all different in many ways both emotionally and physically this is what makes us individuals and so interesting, many of our most endearing qualities come from these differences. We like, even

4

admire, people who are classed as characters or slightly eccentric, if they decide to be reclusive or wear odd clothing, then society accepts their decision without too much questioning. I should make it clear at this point those eccentrics make a choice to act the way they do and don't care what people think. People with Asperger's do care what people think of them and try very hard to conform, they just do not make the connection as to why people think they behave differently. However, if these differences are too exaggerated and do not conform to society's expected boundaries of acceptability, if they don't follow the 'rules', then the person starts to become judged unacceptable and either expected to change to fit in or become ostracised and therefore isolated. But they are just different and should be accepted as just that, rather than be expected to change their fundamental make up so they are no longer 'offensive' to society! As long as they are not hurting anyone then whose business is it but theirs? Unfortunately it is not that simple; society is, and people are, extremely judgemental, we expect people who are considered different from us, who offend our sensibilities, to change their behaviours and beliefs to fit in with our perceived correct codes of conduct. We find it difficult to cope with people who stand out from the crowd because they do, or say, things that do not follow expected social niceties, making people around them feel uncomfortable or embarrassed and unsure how to react. Max doesn't feel he can comment on this subject as there are too many opinions and variables to take into consideration. Everyone is judgemental; it is human nature to put people into boxes.

"If it is to be accepted (embraced, welcomed would be preferable) that people with AS are certainly equal to NT's, if not surpassing them in many qualities - and, surely this is an ethos that should be adopted sooner

5

rather than later - then it seems to me that the next logical step would be to recognise that responsibilities lie just as much with the NT [Neuro Typical] population, as with those with AS to adjust NT behaviour in order to make social situations less stressful and more bearable to people with AS.....How many NT's would make the effort to change their very selves in such a fundamental manner? No wonder so many individuals with AS become reclusive, withdrawn - simply to avoid the NT world that is so potentially (and actually) damaging to their selves and their way of being". Asperger Syndrome & Social Relationships. Genevieve Edmonds and Luke Beardon 2008.

Chapter 3

A brief history of how we met

I first met Max through a cadet organisation, the Sea Cadets. It was about eight weeks after my eldest son joined the junior cadets and they needed some help so I volunteered; not long after this I met Max who worked with the older senior cadets. My first impression was that he was extremely smart, professional and held in high regard. He had been with the cadet organisation for many years so was relaxed and talkative. Everyone seemed to get on well with him as many of them had grown up with him. For me it was rather like being the outsider at a family gathering. I would see him once a month after cadets finished as that was when the younger cadets paraded with the older ones. I liked his witty character and the fact that he would stand up for himself when necessary. Two months after my son joined, the unit went away on camp and I went with the juniors, Max went with the seniors. This was a weeklong camp and Max taught the juniors sailing during part of the week. It was the first time I saw him instructing and I loved the natural way he had with the cadets. They felt safe and tried their hardest to improve so that Max would be impressed with them. In the evenings Max would be found leading games or helping the older cadets with their seamanship skills. He was on their wavelength and this impressed me. He could talk to them in great depth about all the latest computer games and films and would sit completely engrossed watching DVD's that the cadets had chosen.

About a year after joining cadets I decided to start working with the seniors as well as the juniors, and did one night a week with both then two with the seniors and one with the juniors. Max was seconded to juniors as two staff had left

7

suddenly and we needed experienced staff. This meant that we were seeing each other three times a week and I was able to get to know him far better. We specialised in, and taught the same subjects to the cadets which meant that we seemed to be attending the same weekend training courses. It was at these weekends that we got to know each other much better.

I was initially attracted to Max because he was non-conformist and gentle. He didn't seem to feel the need to live up to the silly 'He man' macho behaviour that people seem to think all women want. In fact after a very violent first marriage that was the last thing I wanted. There was, I thought, a lot more to him than he let people see, "hidden depths", a term used by Gisela Slater Walker in 'An Asperger Marriage'. In fact the more I got to know him and the more he let me in, the more I realised that there was indeed a lot more to him than he allowed anyone to see. Over the next eight years we developed a strong friendship and when I split up from my second husband, Max provided me with support giving me black and white advice, no emotional stuff just simple advice, unlike other friends who would give pros and cons to each question I asked. We became close over the next few months; he was my rock always there when I needed him.

When I decided to take my three youngest children on holiday to Spain, he was the logical choice to ask to come with me. All the children knew him, and liked him, and I needed a man to come with me in case there were any problems with taking the boys to the toilet, or to go on theme park rides with the boys which my small daughter would not be allowed on. When I asked him he agreed and in the weeks leading up to the holiday it seemed logical for us to become a couple. It was viewed with surprise and not very positively at cadets, although this seemed illogical at the time, I now realise that there was a degree of jealousy involved as several of them were very fond of him and this relative newcomer, me, had 'managed' to win his affections.

"A man with Asperger syndrome is often attracted to a woman based on the fact that she finds him attractive, and this seems to be more important to him than any feelings of sexual attraction he may have towards her. Specialist counsellor and researcher Maxine Aston found that men with Asperger syndrome were more attracted to a woman who clearly showed that she was attracted to him. This came from their need to be liked, approved of and needed – maybe following a lifetime of rejection. She also found that men with Asperger syndrome were attracted to women who were strong, nurturing and showed excellent social abilities". Asperger syndrome in Adults. Dr Ruth Searle 2010.

When I asked Max what had initially attracted him to me he said *"your arse"*, I can clearly remember not long after I had joined cadets going up the stairs and hearing a voice behind me saying "nice arse" I was flattered, as for years I had not felt attractive or desirable in any way and this comment took me back to days when I did feel attractive and sexy. Max also said, *"I found you visually attractive although I never saw a relationship, I liked you as a friend. I don't hold long conversations with anybody and what helped with you was that you did most of the talking and I can listen. I am good at working things out and offering the best advice, in my opinion, on practical stuff. I just found you a nice person and funny, although I didn't like the fact you were always negative about your relationship. I thought if it was bad then leave that is logical. I didn't fully understand what a difficult position you were in until much later. I didn't really have anyone* *who I could class as a friend, as an adult over the years I have lost the understanding of what a friend is. John was a friend but he was also my guide through his Buddhist teachings. It was John who suggested I took a trip to the coast to find a job; this seemed to be a logical place to look since I was a sailing instructor. In reality during that trip I did a lot of thinking about whom I was and what I wanted out of life. I came back and told Robert, my long standing 'friend' at Sea Cadets, that I would no longer be the butt of his jokes and if he tried it again I would put him in his place. We were on a sailing course at Weymouth when he next tried to make fun of me in front of the adult trainees. I turned the joke on him and said, I told you I would not put up with it anymore. Although the word 'joke' is not a useful one for me as I only saw the behaviour as confusing. Later his wife commented that I had changed. Before John and the journey I was ignorant. What Robert did to me I didn't understand, but after John I suddenly got it, my biggest mistake was naivety and John made me realize this, I saw that what Robert had been doing to me for so many years was wrong. I thought I understood, but over the years I have been s**t on so many times that I lost interest and didn't trust anyone. I only ever had one friend at a time and that was enough. I had conversations with you Annie that I found easy to have, which I didn't often experience with people, but that wasn't it. I felt you were so good looking you had everything that I was looking for, and when I saw your bottom as you went up the stairs in front of me I just couldn't help saying something. I guess I discovered that you were patient although I didn't fully understand this, because when you are on your own you don't have to justify your behaviour, but I found you would tolerate my behaviour. I never regarded myself as patient, I never had to be, but you were".*

I read with interest Sarah Hendrichx's comment about thinking Keith was a Buddhist.

"I thought Keith was some kind of Buddhist; he was so self-sufficient and didn't seem to need the social approval that most people do." 'Asperger Syndrome – a love story' Sarah Hendrickx and Keith Newton 2007

Max's first major life change happened when he met John, a Buddhist, whilst he was doing a cleaning job, they became friends and John took Max under his wing and enlightened him. This man recognised something in Max and encouraged him to improve himself; consequently he went to university and completed an Honours degree in Developmental Psychology, no mean feat for someone who is very dyslexic. Max's route into university was quite accidental. He knew he wanted to improve himself but the rest was almost Karma. Max had fostered a teenager and the boy died not long after he returned to care. *"I couldn't figure out why he died. I felt all he needed was practical care, but this was not enough as I discovered"*. Max needed answers, an understanding, and a reason why it went wrong. *"I wanted to learn more about the psychology behind his behaviour so my brother, Stephen, gave me a book on basic psychology. I didn't find the answer I was looking for but rather a subject that I became fascinated with. The book was very basic but I thought it was fascinating even though the reason for reading it, Joshua, was gone I found I had a fascination for why people ticked; I had never had any reasons or answers before, it opened up a whole new avenue. My brother told me there was a course for adults at the college. It was an access to higher education course and I really wanted to know more about psychology. I went for an interview and it never occurred to me that this initial course was aimed at people wanting to go on to university; I was just focussed on finding out more information. At the interview they asked me what sort of books I read, fiction or factual. I told them that I was only interested in factual books and didn't enjoy fiction at all, all I wanted was factual information; I wanted to learn about psychology. I was offered a place on the course and when I went to the induction meeting in September I found out that this was an access to university course. I passed the course and was offered a place at university to study developmental psychology".*

In his first few days at university he had to write a story about why and how he came to be taking the course; with candles under the table for light and heat, because he couldn't afford electric, he wrote about how he got to university. The story started with the candles under the desk, and ended with the candles, it came full circle. He lacked confidence in his writing abilities, and at school he had never explored these avenues properly because he found them so difficult with his, as then, undiagnosed dyslexia. He gave the story to a friend to read and she started crying, she said it was so heartfelt it wasn't just about how he ended up at university, it was about his life and she found it very emotional. He said, "*I didn't feel it was, it was just about the mistake I had made ending up at college, which had all started from Joshua's death and the fact that I couldn't figure out why he had died and wanted answers and not a pre university course. I felt all he had needed was emotional care so wanted information on the subject. I wanted the information they had and so I really got into university without meaning to, it was a bit of a mistake and things just followed on from there*".

During the first year he struggled with the essays and reading requirements and his tutor suggested that he was tested for dyslexia. He had a pre-test and as a result of the findings, was sent to a psychologist, she asked him a lot of questions and then asked him if he minded if she did a slightly longer test which would take four hours. He agreed and during those hours he was asked to perform many tasks ranging from answering questions, ordering pictorial cards into a story and many more, most of which Max felt had no bearing on ascertaining a diagnosis of dyslexia. Sometime later he was asked to go to London for another assessment to determine what aids would be most beneficial, he was given a computer, extended library cards, so he could keep short loan books out longer, and a specialist tutor. It was at one of his weekly meetings with his tutor that his autism was mentioned. They were discussing the psychologists report, his tutor said, "well she has definitely diagnosed you with dyslexia, but how do you feel about being diagnosed with autism?" He couldn't take it in, the psychologist had obviously assumed that Max knew he was autistic and of course he did not. The dyslexia was one thing and he had gone to get the test results for dyslexia, the autism was a complete shock, one which he refused to acknowledge. His tutor saw his distress and horror and told him that he could have that part of the report taken out, which is what Max wanted, so the tutor arranged it.

His Mum would not acknowledge that Max was dyslexic; she said he was just forgetful, he has told me that, *"she was very protective; she always made lists specifically for me because she knew I was different. Even as an adult she would be waiting for me to come back from the shops as she knew I would have forgotten something"*. Max never told her about the Autism. She was incredibly proud of Max as he was the first one in his family to go to university. After leaving University Max went to work for the Autistic society and, against John's suggestions, became involved in the cadet organisation again. John had thought that the cadets was stifling Max and holding him back. I am very grateful that Max ignored the advice otherwise we would not have met. It was Karma, meant to be!

Maxine Aston, 2003 "gentleness and non-sexual nature of AS men was an important factor in initial attraction." Asperger's in love. "Some of the NT women that I have been in dialogue with had at sometimes in their lives endured some form of abuse. For some, this was due to a dysfunctional upbringing and for others, a previous partner who was abusive. These women had been the victims of circumstances that were out of their control. Most had been emotionally abused and some physically and sexually abused as well. When they met their partners, they recalled how comfortable and safe they felt validated, worthy and very safe; they felt that they were in control."

I had been married twice before I married Max; he has never been married before.

My first marriage was emotionally, physically and sexually abusive and I certainly recognised a very gentle non - sexual side to Max. In the years I had known him before we became a couple I never once saw him disrespect a woman or in fact anyone. He was not sexual or suggestive in any of the interactions I witnessed with other women. He always treated them with respect and chivalry. He was fun to be with, everyone enjoyed his company and he could talk confidently and with authority on a wide range of subjects. Women of all ages adored him and pampered him, at social functions they would gravitate towards him just enjoying his easy nature. Men respected him and his vast knowledge and experience, frequently asking for his advice and input which he gave concisely. He would always fight his corner if someone tried to tell him he had made a mistake or forgotten to do something; people often tried to blame him for their own shortfalls which he would not allow, telling them in no uncertain terms that it was they who had made the mistake and not him. Yet underlying this I witnessed a fragile and confused person, he seemed, at times, out of his depth.

My second marriage produced five wonderful children but, in the main, was devoid of emotional and physical support. I was in essence a single mother as my husband worked very long hours and seemed unable to take responsibility as a father or husband. We grew apart very soon after we were married. This was, I think, mainly because when we first met I was very fragile and not really the person I had been before my first marriage. My personality had been destroyed by the years of abuse and, as I started to regain my true self, my second husband no longer fulfilled my social and emotional needs and I was not the quiet introvert that he had married. Once the children started to come along I felt trapped and unable to walk away from him, I had so many responsibilities, the children, a responsible and demanding career and a home to run. It is the age old problem and one which I didn't tackle for far too many years. Once I made the decision and left him I couldn't believe that I hadn't done it years before, although, had I walked out then I probably wouldn't have met and eventually fallen in love with Max.

Asperger's in Love. "One man said Asperger's syndrome became the bogeyman, the demon; it became responsible for all the problems they had now and in the past. It often comes as a tremendous relief to have a reason and a hanger to blame."

This is not always the case; the sufferer has to accept that he or she has the condition, and accept that they do not react to situations in the same way as non Asperger's people do. They have to be prepared to listen to their partners, and understand that they want to help and their comments and advice are not criticisms just intended to help. The non Asperger partner has to realise that it is very hard to come to terms with Asperger's syndrome and its implications, so they have to tread carefully and choose their words with care. Asperger's sufferers are very particular and sensitive to the way sentences are put together. This sensitivity is heightened when they feel they are being criticised.

When Max told me he was 'Autistic', his words, I was shocked and surprised. He told me very early on in the relationship when we were discussing going on holiday together. I was the first girlfriend he had ever told and the more I learnt, the sorrier I felt for previous girlfriends and the more I realised that he had felt a special connection to me. He had never outwardly behaved in a way that would suggest he was very different from others and had kept everything well controlled. It was as if the Asperger's was invisible. Many Asperger's sufferers function 'well' in society, they are deemed quirky or different but often no one would think they were on the Autistic scale.

I needed to research. Like so many people I had heard horror stories about kids being disruptive and destructive, how they had destroyed families and had to go into special schools. My only experience of Autism was the son of a friend of mine, who had sudden violent outbursts of rage and violence, had poor communication skills and very few, if any, social skills. He was a very difficult and withdrawn child who showed his mum no affection at all. I was vaguely aware that there were varying levels of Autism and that Asperger's was a high end functioning level, still on the Autistic scale but less detectable. I am a real book person and once I found out that Max was Autistic, I felt that if our relationship was going to last then I needed to know as much as I could about the condition. In the first instance he had painted a terrible and brutal picture of himself. It was a damming description explained to me over about thirty minutes, he said, *"I have no emotions and will never commit to a relationship so don't think that we will ever have a future together. All of my previous relationships have ended very quickly because they were too difficult so I ended them. I am hard, cold and prefer my own company to that of others"*. This was a curious conversation since at the time I was cuddled up on his lap after a very enjoyable, romantic evening. We had both had a few drinks and he was very relaxed, which is why I think he felt it necessary to tell me about his condition at that precise moment. Had I been of fainter heart and not known him for such a long time, I would have walked away right then, but I felt there was a lot more to him and I was convinced that it couldn't be as bad as he had said. Ever the optimist!

Once I started to research I discovered that there was lots of information on children and adolescents with Autism and how to parent them successfully. I also discovered that there were different degrees of the syndrome.

I found a few books that were written about adult relationships and found them useful each one offered an insight into a specific relationship. There were some areas that I could identify with and relate them to our situation, but there were others that were completely alien. The main benefit I found was that they helped me ignore the criticism or precise and exacting demands from Max, and understand that they were not said with any intended malice. Initially I read these in secret as I felt that Max might think I was prying. After about a year I started to read a book in front of him 'Asperger Syndrome- a love story'. Max spotted it and asked what it was about I told him and that I had been reading around the subject, he was very interested. As we chatted it turned out that I knew far more about it than Max. He asked me what I was reading about and I decided to read a couple of relevant passages to him, ones that had similarities to our relationship. E.g. STIMS and bluntness, both of these are discussed in later chapters. He was amazed as he could identify with what Keith was expressing. He was interested so I continued; of course Max could not identify with everything I read and I explained that this was very typical of Asperger's as there were so many variances. He said that the diagnosis had been mentioned after he had been tested for Dyslexia at university, this was completely a new concept and not one that he could take on board or understand so refused to believe or accept it. Max's image of autism was a very negative one similar to many other people's views, so he walked away and blanked the diagnosis.

"The process of diagnosis is very stressful and painful to accept, especially when you have had a mainstream life throughout existence. Suddenly when you get the diagnosis you have to learn to accept a new identity, except it is technically something that you already are but not known of." Asperger Syndrome and Social Relationships. Genevieve Edmonds and Luke Beardon 2008.

Having researched extensively it was clear to me that Max had Asperger's syndrome. In the early stages of our relationship I felt that I was constantly treading on eggshells, picking the right words and terminology, thinking before I spoke, not expecting or demanding anything and always being there for him, pampering him. I hoped that he would text or call when we were apart just to say, "Hi", although soon realised that this was not going to happen. When we were apart he enjoyed his space and felt no need to contact me as he knew when we were meeting again. I, on the other hand, just wanted to hear his voice, an irrational reassurance that things were still ok. I would initiate the occasional text finding some rather ridiculous reason that I now know he saw through instantly, I am therefore rather lucky that he was genuinely interested in the possibilities of a relationship, otherwise he would have finished it immediately.

Soon after we started going out he decided that he needed to retreat into his 'bubble' or 'cave', take time out. He told me that I should not contact him for three days and if I tried he would ignore my texts. I was mortified but tried to understand, secretly hoping that it was just him saying it and he would contact me sooner. By day two I thought it was all over because there had been no contact. I was waiting outside the children's school around three o'clock when I received a text from him. It read, "*I miss you*", I replied with a very short text, "I miss you too, Happy Birthday". I got no reply but it raised my spirits and I resisted my urge to try and prolong our conversation. The next day he contacted me and asked if we could meet, I readily agreed and we had a lovely belated birthday celebration. That evening we saw each other at Cadets and I felt great, but we had kept our relationship secret from cadet staff as it was in the early stages and felt that it would not be very sensible to make it known so early on, particularly since my children attended the unit, so were unable to continue our lovely chat. The following weekend we talked about his time out and he really appreciated that I had not pestered him and had understood his need to be alone. He told me that if I had tried to make contact he would have known that I didn't understand him and our relationship would be over. This incident has never happened since for which I am very grateful, however, if he needed time out I would have no hesitation in agreeing to it and abiding by the rules for as long as it took.

Everyone who knows us say that we are the perfect couple, so loving and happy. It's amazing what people miss, no-one knows that Max has Asperger's Syndrome and don't realise what a daily challenge it is for both of us to maintain our relationship. But we have a great thing going and it is well worth the effort to keep it so wonderful. The great thing is that the more we discover and talk about, the better and deeper our relationship becomes.

There is a great analogy made by Rudy Simone in 22 things a woman must know if she loves a man with Asperger's Syndrome 2009.

"..an Asperger man is like a rock and the woman who loves him is water, moulding herself around him. As a rock is shaped by water, he will be shaped by her influence, but ever so slowly. She will be better off being gentle and persistent, for, if she comes on strong like a wave, she'll only break herself upon his immovable frame time and again until there is nothing left of her and she is spent."

Although living with someone with AS is definitely challenging on a daily basis because, no matter how well you think you know the person and understand the condition; there are always those unexpected 'shut downs', moments of strange behaviour and other such things. These challenges are at least balanced by, and in our case outweighed by, the positives that we have. These include an open and totally honest relationship, complete loyalty, spontaneity, fun and laughter to mention but a few. It is very well worth working at for these benefits.

"Asperger Syndrome is not a problem among other people with Asperger Syndrome – it is only a problem for people who are classed as neurotypical and are unable to understand how information is processed differently in atypical individuals. A change of perspective is all that is needed for people to see the many benefits of knowing and loving someone who has Asperger syndrome, rather than dwelling on the problems." Asperger Syndrome in Adults. Dr Ruth Searle 2010.

Chapter 4

Max's childhood memories

When Max was a child he had a large number of hearing tests, this was because he seemed not to hear what people were saying to him; in fact he has now realized that it was a case of comprehension as his hearing was perfect. Sounds seem to get amplified and voices grated together until they make no sense at all so when things got too difficult for him he would just 'tune out' to avoid the stress. This is very common amongst Asperger's sufferers and is often called 'selective deafness'. His Mum didn't know this so naturally thought he hadn't heard what was being said. He recalls one hearing test where he was shut in a soundproof booth and they played tunes in his ears, when he heard each one he had to press a button; he found this tremendous fun shut in his own musical bubble. This made such an impression on him that he would love to build his own sound proof room and experience this feeling again; it seemed that the silence had a sound of its own and this has made a lasting impression on him;

"There was no confusion at all, just me and nothing".

"I was always injuring myself and Mum would take me to the hospital for X-rays, stitches, etcetera. I think I was just accident prone, I was always playing outside searching rubbish dumps for interesting things and loved exploring derelict houses and other such interesting places. I remember on one visit the nurse who was treating me told me that if I came back to the hospital again then I would have to stay there forever. This really scared me because I didn't want to live in a hospital. A few weeks later I injured myself again and Mum said I had to go to the hospital, I screamed the place down but she still took me; I

was sure that I would not be coming home again but I did. That was confusing".

When Max was about 11 his Mum planned a birthday party for him with a slight difference because she could only invite one friend for him, to make it more like a party she combined it with his younger twin sister's party.

"Mum recognized that I didn't really have friends of my own except Paul, but wanted me to have a party so when she arranged a birthday party for my twin sisters she told me that it was for me. When it happened, and all my sister's friends turned up, I realized that it was their party and not mine because only Paul came for me. I was ok with this because I only ever had one friend and it was wonderful that she had recognized this and put the party on so I could experience this. I hijacked my sister's party but that was ok as well."

"I loved playing football but was always looking in from outside the fence. I had no connection with the social aspect of the game, I just loved kicking the ball, being in control and delivering it to the goal. It was nothing about team work, I did it for me. They wouldn't allow me to play, they never asked me to join in, but I noticed that if you just stood there long enough in the middle of the players, eventually the ball would come towards you and you got into the game. Once you had chosen the goal you were heading for that was the team you were on and everyone just sort of accepted it. In one game I wanted to score a goal so I got the ball and ran from one end of the pitch to the other where I kicked the ball at the goal, I missed but I had been totally focused and absorbed with the ball".

"Another ball game I really loved was using a medicine ball. You had to get the ball from one end of the court to

*the other without it leaving the ground. This meant you
had to dribble it along the ground. I never viewed this as a
team game although it was meant to be. I was one of the
shortest in the class but very fast and agile so always won.
Like the football I focused and succeeded alone".*

*"I loved Gymnastics, I was very agile and flexible so was
very good at it especially since it was a solitary activity, so
I didn't have to involve anyone else. I just got on and did
my own thing, wonderful".*

*"Soon after going to secondary school, my friend Paul told
me about sex! I can remember saying, 'No way; that's
impossible, people don't do that to each other'. I was
horrified and didn't believe a word of it. Consequently I
denied all of it and told him it was impossible and he
should go away".*

*"My first 'crush' or sexual attraction was with a girl in my
year, year seven. She used to sing a song that had the
lyrics, 'do you want to cha cha cha, do you want to be cha
cha cha', I used to say 'yeah'. It was a game and I loved
to play it, she was playing it with me and I enjoyed the
game. She was the most mature girl in year seven, I was
very naïve but knew she was being sexual and I enjoyed
her attention".*

*"I really didn't have any friends apart from Paul but there
were a group of oddballs, myself among them who seemed
to gravitate towards each other. We were not friends but
shared a mutual problem, we were on our own, some
through choice and others because no one would play with
them. One of these boys was called Wang and I did talk to
him occasionally. He was a small Chinese boy who didn't
say a lot. One day a large boy who would be in a special
school nowadays decided to give Wang a bear hug around*

his neck. I noticed that Wang could not breathe because the boy was squeezing so tightly. He was oblivious of his own strength and the danger he was putting Wang in. I went over to him and told him to stop because Wang couldn't breathe. He just looked at me and grunted, not in an angry way just because he knew I was there. I told him that I would have to stop him if he didn't let go of Wang, still he didn't stop so I warned him again and then hit him as hard as I could, this had no effect on him at all I had to hit him again to make him break his hold and allow Wang to breathe again. I knew what he was doing was wrong because you do not hurt anyone and the only way I could stop him was to use violence which I hate".

"My favourite childhood toys were cardboard boxes and curtains. I could hide in a box all day with a few small holes punched in it so I could watch people going by and they couldn't see me. I really enjoyed this and could do it all the time. Curtains were also great fun; I would hide behind them watching everything going on around me without having to interact with anyone. This carried on until I was about twelve or thirteen. When I joined Sea Cadets I seemed to need to do this less as there were lots of rules and routines which I liked and this helped me.
Other toys included a matchbox car, 'loop the loop', 'flight deck' a game that involved landing a plane on a ships flight deck, it didn't work too well but I did enjoy it a lot and a pull and go motorbike. My very favourite was a musical wind up Fischer Price television, it had a prism effect which wasn't very good but I loved to play with it for hours and hours watching the pictures scroll across the screen as the music played. Mum bought it for me and I know that I was a lot older when she got it for me than the toy was intended for, but I really wanted it and it gave me hours and hours of fun".

Chapter 5

Bullying

90% of children with AS have suffered bullying. (Attwood 2006)

Max tended to withdraw into his safety bubble rather than lash out except when defending a cause he felt strongly about. The first time he got into a fight in year seven was when he saw a large child, the school bully, picking on a smaller one in the dinner queue. He wouldn't ever start a fight on purpose, but he would just point out that whatever they were doing was wrong and then, if they didn't accept it and stop, he would *'deal'* with them. One whack and they were down. On this occasion the boy told him that he did karate and to leave him alone so Max hit him and gave him a black eye. Max never started a fight but he would protect people who were being bullied.

"If I think a rule has been broken then I will react accordingly".

When we first started to talk about whether Max was bullied as a child, he initially said that he didn't think that he had been bullied, but over time it has become very apparent both to him, and me, that he was a victim of bullying from childhood and through into adulthood, which at times made his life very miserable because of the confusion and chaos.

"Primary school was ok but secondary school never worked for me. I lived my whole secondary life in fear, every day was filled with fear, and I had never felt this at primary school. I think part of this was because I had lost continuity, there were so many classes to try and find, so

many opinions to listen to and so many people all talking at me. I only had one friend and he was a boy I knew from primary school and who came to my secondary school. I even had to move English classes because Paul and I were put into different ones at first and I couldn't cope with that. My whole life fell apart, school was very lonely. I felt like an outsider at secondary school very on my own. It didn't matter, but I felt trapped, all at sea or like I was in prison, I didn't want to be there at all, I wanted to be at home and safe. I didn't feel like I was being bullied at school, I kept to myself, but I now realise that I was. Everyone was in their friendship groups and I was on my own, I just retreated into my own world because it was safer there. I could hear them calling me names but I would carry on being in my own world, longing for home time. I just sat there watching and very rarely ever interacted, I only did if someone was with me and it was something specific that I wanted to join in with, I never felt a need to join in. I was happy to watch and wait for home time. I really began to understand bullying when I went to college and there I really did experience it. I never had any friends there and saw groups of people chatting and laughing, I was the butt of people's jokes. People laughed at me and about me and although I didn't understand what they were laughing about I just knew they were. I had friends at Cadets which I joined at 13, I joined because my cousin joined and Mum encouraged me to go. I started in army cadets but when a friend there moved to Sea Cadets I copied him and stayed with Sea cadets until I was 18 when I became a member of staff".

I have watched Max interacting with adults in many situations, both prior to our relationship, and since we became a couple. As a result of our conversations and discussions about his life and the information from books on Asperger's, he has started to realised that some actions and behaviours he endured from people he considered friends, were in fact unkind and thoughtless. I have witnessed people taking advantage of his good nature, teasing him when his 'innocence' has shown through and being physically aggressive towards him.

I have witnessed him clipped round the ear, on several occasions, by one long standing female friend, someone he trusted and he had even lived with her and her husband when he came back during the holidays whilst at university. This was viewed by other friends of his as acceptable and even funny as if he had asked for it. He never understood why she did this or what he had done to warrant it. This action stopped as soon as they became aware that Max and I were a couple, as I am sure they knew that I would not tolerate this sort of behaviour, as I understood that it was bullying, even if Max did not. It had been very hard for me to speak up against these actions prior to this because, although I liked Max a lot, I felt that he would be upset and confused if I had stepped in to stop them without reason. For Max problems have an answer, when there appears to be no answer or no explanation of a particular behaviour, whatever it is, it cannot be dealt with or rationalised. It is the same if you are being bullied you can't deal with it unless you understand it first. He still does not understand their behaviour but accepts that it is wrong. You can't recognise or defend yourself against something that you don't understand or realise is happening. Max would be the first to admit that he could bully but he would argue, though not justify, that it would be through ignorance or anger. He would not feel any emotional need to bully someone just because he could.

"Humans have a habit of embellishing stories each time they tell them to suit the audience".

28

I witnessed several times Max getting quite annoyed while listening to someone at cadets recounting a story, which Max had been part of, and adding bits to make it more interesting or funny. Often this involved something Max might have said or done. Max would say *"it didn't happen like that"* or *"that's not accurate"* and similar such things. The usual recourse was that Max had a bad memory and it was him that was mistaken. Max couldn't understand why they changed the story and twisted his words and then said it was him that was wrong, in effect making out he was the stupid one. They relied on his 'innocence', and at times poor memory, to get away with their stories which, the way they were telling it, generally made them look more interesting than they actually were, and Max look more foolish. They would end up laughing at Max and his supposed antics and not the accurate content of the original story. I know this was true as some of the stories recounted I was witness to, and know that Max's version is far more accurate. Certainly he has a poor memory for names and places but generally he has a good memory for events, although he probably cannot remember how long ago it was or where it happened.

Defensiveness

"Another common problem in communication is defensiveness. This may be at least partly attributed to the fact that many people with AS are bullied all their lives, usually from adolescence on. So even the gentlest attempts at reasoning may at first hit a wall of self-protectiveness. He's been used to being misunderstood and misrepresented all his life. (Being the square peg constantly trying to fit into a round hole and possibly being mocked or condemned for it.)" Rudy Simone. 22 Things a woman should know if she loves a man with Asperger's Syndrome.

Max will often display a defensive stance if I question or dispute something he has said or done. It can be the simplest of things said in passing, or something that was mentioned whilst he was preoccupied and so didn't fully hear it and yet, rather than discuss this rationally, he will go on the defence saying I am wrong and that he is right and I have not understood what he said or did. Generally I will not pursue this any further and when he is ready he will bring it up and we can have a more rational discussion; but it is incredibly hard to back down all the time and allow Max to be 'right'. There are many occasions during a week when I have to concede to being incorrect rather than risk a confrontation which would really distress Max. He genuinely believes that he is correct and yet I know that often he has misheard something that has been said, or misinterpreted an emotional inflection and so got it in the wrong context. I do not pursue these things but it is emotionally exhausting. What I keep in mind is that this is only a very small part of our relationship and if I can cope with these conflicts, not take them personally and try to explain things in simple 'Max speak' then life will be easier. It is still a learning curve and we both have a long way to go but I am sure we will meet somewhere near the middle, hopefully, given time. Max is getting better at discussing his reasons for becoming so defensive and I can understand his reactions much better now. It is more difficult for the children though and we will have to find a way to overcome these problems, although he is more tolerant when he and the children have a conflict. I can usually explain that they are like it because they are still children and therefore more likely to misunderstand what he has said. I, on the other hand, should be accountable for my actions and words.

Chapter 6

Trust

We have a relationship based on total trust and honesty, certainly on my part, and in his own way he trusts me as much as he is able and this is helped because we have good communication. Max says, *"I trust you more than anyone else ever, but I must quantify this and say I don't trust anyone. I know that you will let me down it is human nature, I have given you the highest accolade but I trust no-one because every human I have ever met has let me down, because they do not understand about trust and loyalty and I do not understand about love"*. Because Max and I have an excellent level of communication I trust Max completely. Every decision we need to make is done jointly, we discuss everything and Max has excellent judgement especially where the children are concerned.

This is something that all couples would like to say they have but in most of the relationships I have witnessed there has always been an element of distrust. Some minor and others major. Examples of what I mean are when a wife/girlfriend husband/boyfriend goes out alone with friends, the partner wonders who their partner is chatting to or dancing with. They may say they trust the partner and it is all the others in the club or social gathering, but there is still an element of uncertainty, after all 'it takes two to tango' as they say. I can say, hand on heart, that I totally trust Max. I know that if he no longer wanted me to be his wife he would tell me in his blunt way, and he would not have a problem doing this; it would have been a decision that had been made and needed to be followed through. It wouldn't be flowered up or excuses made it would be direct and to the point. There would certainly be no secret affair dragging on for months until he was found out for two reasons, and these are directly because of his Asperger's. Firstly he does not lie he can see no point in lying and this has been demonstrated in several chapters of the book, and secondly he would be unable to manage two relationships. He finds it hard enough coping with one extra person in his 'bubble', having to cope with the 'demands' of two women would be totally beyond his ability.

It is very important that I know he has Asperger's otherwise some of his behaviour could be construed as evasive or secretive. He doesn't elaborate on information unless I ask him direct questions, so if we had difficulty with communication then I could feel he was not telling me things deliberately, rather than him not realising that I was interested in what he considers daily trivia.

I am one of the very few people who know about his condition and the first person who he has ever allowed into his world. He has told me often that if we split up there would never be anyone else. He says, "*I have allowed you into my life more than anyone else in the world that I have ever known including my mother, sister and even John*". His Asperger's, means that this is an accurate and concise description of the situation. If I were to betray his trust that would be the end of our relationship, there would be no going back no reconciliation it would be over he has made this very clear.

We often go out to clubs together and I feel totally free to talk to anyone knowing that Max is '*ok*' with this. At first this was odd as in all previous relationships I was watched and distrusted, eyes boring into me where ever I went; I would be questioned on my return about my conversations and the people I had talked to. This problem also carried over into my daily life, I worked predominantly with men as a paramedic and would come home and talk about what various colleagues had done in the day, this was viewed with suspicion as most of the names I used were male, my ex-husband wanted to know who they were and how often I worked with them. I very quickly stopped mentioning them. With Max I can talk openly and talk in detail about anyone I have encountered in my day. Max is not jealous, it is an emotion and so *"impossible"* for him to feel, although he understands that people do act strangely as a result of jealousy. It is a great feeling knowing that he trusts me, quite liberating. I don't have to be careful who I talk to or watch what I say to him about male contacts I have made during the day.

In 'Asperger Syndrome-a love story', I notice that Sarah says that Keith is happy if Sarah is in sight.

"He says that he is fine as long as he can see me somewhere in the room. I don't have to be by his side but within sight. I'm not sure why this makes a difference". Keith says, *"It is comforting to know that Sarah is around, for with just a glance across a room she can see and understand my discomfort, and that is enough. It doesn't need to be taken away; just to have her recognise that I'm not at ease is enough. Sarah is not only aware, she actually understands."*

Max is the same, I do not have to be glued to his side all night just be around in case he '*needs*' me.

I feel valued by Max, he is always saying I help him and care for him. He appreciates everything I do, yet he often says he is a '*twat*' because he does not feel he is fulfilling his role as a husband. I have tried reminding him that my previous experiences of what a husband is have not been altogether that good, and that as far as I am concerned he far outweighs them in every way but, as is typical of people with Asperger's, he feels that because he has no understanding of my emotional needs he is somehow failing me. Another aspect is that he has an image firmly imprinted in his head of what a perfect relationship is; this by his nature is one which he has to adhere to and he has set himself very high standards, far higher than the average couple need or expect. It has been put together from images from films depicting ideal couples, or documentaries about relationships which haven't been perfect, listening to the negatives and choosing to follow a different path. I don't think he realises how much I value him and how wonderful and happy he makes me feel, even though I tell him all the time how special and important he is to me and how happy he makes me. I know that there are areas in our relationship which we struggle with, but that is true of all relationships, whether one partner has Asperger's or not, and all successful relationships take effort from both parties. It is not easy but if it is worth it you should fight to maintain it.

If you tell an AS person they are useless or no good at doing something, they will stop doing good stuff altogether because they will believe they are useless at everything. I think that over the years through a series of failed relationships he has come to the conclusion that he is useless so it has become a self-fulfilling prophecy.

"This man had heard so many times how he had failed at meeting his wife's emotional needs that he had stopped trying. This is known as a self-fulfilling prophecy. A long-term negative way of thinking can change how hard we try, and may eventually mean that, because we believe we will fail we do not try at all...If, for example, his partner says that he has been thoughtless he will only consider the

34

word 'thoughtless', and not the context in which it was said. If he considers himself thoughtless then this will simply reinforce his belief about himself. If however, he has already decided that he is a thoughtful person, then what she is saying will be seen purely as criticism, or as her being vindictive or malicious." Asperger's in Love Maxine Aston.

Chapter 7

Self-disclosure

"Although sixty-nine per cent of AS men said they could make some disclosures to their partners, only ten per cent felt they were able to disclose information regarding themselves. This is quite a contradiction to the high level of trust that many men with AS said they had for their partners. It normally follows that if you totally trust someone you are able to talk to him or her about most things and are able to trust them with that information.
Many men said they felt threatened when asked direct questions by their partners and quite suspicious as to why she wanted to know and what she was going to do with the information if they supplied it. One man said that any personal questions from his wife felt like an intrusion. Another said that whatever he told his partner about himself was always used to criticise him at a later date."
Maxine Aston Asperger's in Love.

Being able to trust your partner with personal and private information is very important for couples. It makes the relationship stronger knowing such private details. Max and I certainly have a huge level of trust; we talk constantly discussing all aspects of our relationship. This not only applies to day to day information but also more intimate things. This is an area which I have had a real problem with because of my past relationships. With Max I feel safe enough to discuss even the hardest parts of it. Many of these things have been repressed for years and come to the surface in fits and starts, not in any particular order and usually when we are relaxed in bed close and cuddled up. I feel safe there. I have never spoken to anyone else about them before yet Max allows me to talk without judging me. I know that Max finds the information very hard to understand, firstly because I am talking about things that have happened to me, his wife, and secondly he cannot understand how anyone, particularly a husband, could do such hideous things to another human being, let alone their wife with whom they are supposed to have a close bond. We have a special openness and Max opens up to me about things which have happened to him in the past which have confused or hurt him; yet even now after four years I still do not know how old he is. He tells no one and this is something he has inherited from his mother whose age no one knew until she died. It is a bit like a 'Peter Pan' complex and once someone knows his true age he will become that age. He maintains that he is twenty one and this is his final word on it. Although this is not normally a problem as such and I respect his privacy, in certain circumstances it has caused problems. For example, I tried to claim benefits when I was out of work briefly, because I couldn't give them his DOB, I couldn't claim the benefit. Another rather amusing occasion occurred when we wanted to get married. The registrar asked me questions to verify I knew who Max was. When asked his DOB, I had to explain that he told no one and this was just the way he was. She looked somewhat bemused, but asked me some other questions for verification and then witnessed it for herself when he had to write it down on a form, he shielded it from her and me asking it to be moved from the table when he had finished it so I couldn't see it and in effect nor could he. Interestingly when she asked Max questions about me he was unable to remember my full name until he had a little prompt from her, she told me later that it was usually the man who couldn't remember information about his prospective wife and that is why she always interviewed the woman first. He does say that if I found out what his DOB was he wouldn't want to know that I knew. Friends and family find it odd but I am used to it. If we are phoning the bank and they require verification that they are talking to the right person, I have to leave the room whilst Max gives them his details, then he will hand the phone over to me to continue talking as he doesn't like these types of call. He has told me that I am trusted more than anyone else ever, but there are still some things that I will never know. They are not a problem unless they interfere with finances or similar. Max would say that he trusts me completely but not with certain information, very odd but fairly typical of a large percentage of AS men.

Chapter 8

Understanding social situations

"Someone with Asperger syndrome tends to lack empathy with other people. The ability to show empathy first requires an ability to recognise the emotional state of another person....Although the actions and words used by most people are fundamentally driven by their emotional state, it is perhaps surprising that many people don't necessarily 'spell out' how they are feeling at the time. We therefore need to listen to tone of voice or observe body language such as eye contact, posture, gesture and facial expression....Contrary to common belief, people with Asperger syndrome do not necessarily prefer to be alone – they enjoy social contact, despite the difficulties it might bring". Dr Ruth Searle. *Asperger Syndrome in Adults.* Sheldon Press 2010.

I went to visit my friend to discuss this book and asked Max if he would like to come with me, he asked if I really wanted him to come and, sensing that he was uneasy with the idea, I told him that I was ok with going on my own. Later he told me that he had felt awkward about the whole thing. *"I feel like I am in a test tube, I am the one that is being examined and opened up. I couldn't have sat there and heard you discussing me like some sort of lab rat. I know you have discussed the book and Tracy has read the manuscript, but I am a very private person and wouldn't have been comfortable being part of the discussion".* I thoroughly understood the dilemma; he is able to discuss things with me as we talk all the time about our relationship, how the Asperger's affects it and ways to ease the burden for both of us, but to discuss it with a relative stranger is a very difficult concept for him. He is obviously aware that once the book is published it will be accessible to a vast audience but these are not people he knows or ever will, they are anonymous and therefore of no importance. Tracy on the other hand is someone he meets occasionally socially and so she would see him in a different light, one which he would find difficult. He can blank the fact that we have talked, but if he had been a part of it then that would make a huge difference.

Communication

"Given that seventy per cent of communication is unspoken, the remaining thirty per cent does not leave them with much information to get by on."
Asperger's in Love. Maxine Aston

Max's command of language is excellent although, if he has misheard a word initially or it has been used incorrectly when he heard it, he may continue using it in this fashion. If such an occasion arises I will correct him, in private of course. One word is the abbreviation for application when used to discuss downloads on an iphone he says 'apts' instead of 'apps'. Sometimes his use of language or choice of words is strange to people, often he cannot remember the obvious words and uses less common ones, they are still correct but unusual. His ability to talk, apparently comfortably, in a variety of social situations is helped by his use of language. He is able to talk to anyone no matter what their background or social standing. He has no interest in their background and is not fazed by it. I think that his ability to mimic speech patterns also helps as he does not come across too 'posh' or too 'common' which can be intimidating to some people. In these situations he uses language which is appropriate and easily understood by the listener putting them at ease, and so making the conversation easier for both parties.

He finds it easier to communicate with children because they are simple and straightforward, *"I really get them"*. Kids appreciate his honest and simplistic approach. He sees what they are saying and cuts out all the "rubbish" or adult assumptions and thinking.

"Kids have less confusion or social stuff behind them, they just do it because they want to, most things kids do are very logical to them, even if it doesn't fit with the norm or adult viewpoint, they have a rational explanation for it."

"There is also research and clinical evidence that the person may have knowledge about other people's minds, but they are unable to apply this knowledge effectively (Bowler 1992). They can 'intellectualise' what a person may be thinking or feeling, but cannot recognise when such skills are necessary to the situation. This has been called a lack of central drive for coherence *– that is, an inability to see the relevance of different types of knowledge to a particular problem (Frith and Happe 1994)".*

Max observes behaviour and has taught himself how to read inflections etc, and where they usually occur in human interactions and can do this reasonably well most of the time. He has no idea why they do it, but understands that they almost certainly will in a variety of situations.

When they do not, he looks for another path and can predict what their next sentence or type of behaviour should be. He finds this ability very useful because people are quite stereotypical and usually follow his predictions. If they don't it confuses him and he looks for reasons for the new response. *"People are too confusing!"* Max is aware that there are multiple meanings of words, phrases and pictures depending upon inflections used or context they are used in, however, he as all AS sufferers will use the literal one as his default.

Max's job involves interviewing families about their child's attendance at school and factors affecting this, he has to get to the bottom of some very complex situations. He expects them to reply in a certain way to a question and knows they are hiding something when they do not, his 'sixth sense' kicks in, he looks for reasons and asks more searching questions until he feels the truth is out. He remembers things they have said previously and notices subtle inconsistencies, and questions them to get to the truth. He is very direct, and because he doesn't have the usual constraints of social niceties, he asks very direct and searching questions in order to get to the truth. It is a bit like solving a mystery following clues and getting to the truth. There is a format for success and Max uses it to great effect. He is extremely well respected at work and has received many accolades from colleagues, professionals and schools he works with because of his thoroughness and successes. A real positive, for someone who struggles so hard with daily life.

Max has difficulty with nonverbal communication finding it especially hard to work out eye contact, body language and facial expressions. He particularly does not like eye contact especially if it lasts more than a few seconds; it makes him feel uncomfortable as if people are staring at him. He can maintain it with me for a little longer than he can with other people but looks away when he gets uneasy.

There was an incident when I was practicing an assembly for school in front of Max. As he was the only audience I found myself staring at him. I did not notice at first but his behaviour started to change, he started to become silly and challenging like a child. From my discussion with Max later, I realised that he was so disturbed by the staring that he would try anything to stop it.

Literal use or translation of language

Max always defaults to the literal, it is a bit like translating word for word, He is getting better at converting to the literal he describes it like this, "*It is like someone listening to a foreign language such as French, you convert it to English. A French person wouldn't have to do this, they naturally understand it. I have to constantly convert to the literal, it is as if I have heard it in French and have to convert it to English which is very tiring and frustrating. I don't want to default to anything but my brain is hard wired to do that, it's exhausting and I just wish people would use the literal*".

An example of Max's literal translation is the following: "Are you hungry?" "*Yes*" "What would you like?" "*Food*". Most people would suggest something such as soup or a sandwich when asked what they would like. These scenarios are made more difficult as Max has a great sense of humour and often uses wordplay, so what seems to be a literal answer to a question is also humorous. We spend a lot of time playing out scenarios where I try to reword a question which demands an answer that I can use. So I now ask him what type of food he would like, this may get the response "*edible food*" or something more useful! It sounds very frustrating, but you do get used to it and can devise ways to illicit the desired information quicker if you don't feel like playing.

His boss has fallen into the trap of his literal translation and inadvertently offered him a solution. She would constantly ask him if he would like a cup of tea to which he would answer, "No", because he didn't want tea, if she had asked if he had wanted a cup of coffee he would have said yes. She would make a tea and then Max would go and make his coffee. She obviously saw this happen and one day said, "All you need to do is tell me you would prefer a coffee when I ask about tea and I will make you one".

A similar literal scenario is described by Gisela Slater Walker

"Chris's reaction to language is inclined to be literal, so a question, 'Do you want a tea or a coffee?' will be answered 'Yes'. The non autistic person would understand from the context in which the question had been asked, that the real meaning of the question was 'Which would you prefer, a tea or coffee?' Again, it is easy to interpret the unhelpful answer as being deliberately obscure, when this is not the case at all. It can often be Chris's humour, he enjoys the concept that there are two meanings, one literal and one implied, in much of everyday speech, though I suspect that the literal response is always the first to come to his mind." An Asperger Marriage. Gisela and Christopher Slater-Walker.

Another funny literal interpretation was soon after we started sleeping together, I told him that I would like him to cuddle me for a minute before he went to sleep. He said that he could do that. That night we got into bed and he dutifully cuddled up behind me. It was lovely and I was just getting comfortable when he said, *"Is that a minute?"* I was amazed and tried to explain that I had not meant literally one minute it was just a figure of speech. He asked me why I hadn't said that in the first place and wanted to know how long he was supposed to cuddle me for. We resolved it by deciding that when he had had enough he should roll over, this has worked very well ever since.

Theory of Mind. From the age of around four years, children understand that other people have thoughts, knowledge, beliefs and desires that will influence their behaviour. People with Asperger's Syndrome appear to have some difficulty conceptualising and appreciating the thoughts and feelings of another person. For example, they may not realise that their comment could cause offense or embarrassment or that an apology would help to repair the person's feelings. Tony Attwood, Asperger's Syndrome. A guide for parents and professionals. 1998

Conversations

Max and I have wonderful and in depth conversations and he can also talk in social situations often at length on a variety of subjects. He will become quiet if it is a subject he has no interest in or little knowledge of, and may well try to change the subject matter to one he considers much more interesting if he is bored. In extreme cases he will walk away from boring or tiresome conversations. Having said that, he is fascinated by learning new things and will listen until he feels that the person has exhausted their knowledge base, or is just talking for the sake of it. If Max feels that the information is flawed he will point that out, even if he has only a limited knowledge of the subject matter. He is very good at putting his point across but it is often said quite forcefully, he lets the other person say their piece and then when it starts to conflict with Max's opinion, he will interrupt and '*put them right*'. Max does not seem to understand when it is appropriate to interrupt a conversation without being rude, he will just step in when he has something to say and not wait for the usual pauses in the dialogue.

Once in full flow Max hates to be interrupted and will say something like, *"If I can just finish what I was saying"* or *"when you're ready I would like to continue with my sentence"*. It means that I should shut up and let him carry on. Often I have tried to interrupt when I want him to clarify a particular point, or I am trying to add my view point on what he has just said, rather than change the subject or dispute what he has just said. I find it difficult to remember what I have wanted to say by the end of the conversation, and feel the need to get my point in at the appropriate time but Max really hates this.

If I have initiated the conversation then a completely different set of rules come into play. I will start chatting and I will see a frustrated look coming over his face, this is usually because I am adding in background information and so, in his mind, deviating from the main point of the story. This will result in him saying, *"Get to the point"* so I have to finish the story without any further explanations or embellishments. The extra bits I have been adding are usually, in my opinion, useful to Max for example, if I am talking about a person I will try to remind him where he met them last or the connection I have with them so he can see the relevance of the story. They tend not to be put in to flower up the story, although I know I do waffle a bit and get side-tracked when telling stories! He will also interrupt me mid-sentence saying things like, *"we will come back to that"* or *"hold that thought"*, and start talking about something that has just occurred to him, often an idea that has been triggered by a word or thought that I have mentioned and his mind has latched onto it and sent him off on a tangent. It is pointless trying to return to my conversation when he stops me, as he is focussed on his thought and would not hear what I was saying anyway. By the time he has finished what he needed to say I have usually forgotten what I was saying.

"...one of the potentially infuriating aspects of Asperger's syndrome is a tendency to interrupt. The person has difficulty identifying the cues for when to start talking (i.e. a momentary pause, the end of the topic of conversation or the body language and eye contact that indicate 'your turn'). They may also not appreciate the effect of interrupting on the flow of conversation or the feelings of the other person. The skill of interrupting without causing offence or disruption is quite complex and difficult to explain," Tony Attwood. Asperger's Syndrome. A guide for parents and professionals.

These interruptions, although not usually socially acceptable and often considered rude, are probably what many of us would secretly like to do but don't because we know that it is considered socially unacceptable and do not want to be seen as rude, so we listen to endless drivel, probably filled with inconsistencies and inaccuracies, until the speaker is finished. We would not criticise someone's opinion or point out that they were wrong in front of others because that would be rude and thoughtless. So often the black and white thinking of a person with Asperger's, and their poor understanding of social etiquette can save them and those around them from hours of tedious conversation. To counter this from a partner's point of view, I am often very conscious that someone might take offence at the interruptions or corrections, so make every effort to prevent too many such situations arising by diverting him in some way. I can usually spot when he is starting to get irritated with the dialogue or he has already started to make comments, and will suggest he gets some drinks, or simply wait for the accepted interruption point and make our excuses to move away. Max is also getting much better at taking cues from me when I sense him about to interrupt and change the subject or dispute a piece of information. A little squeeze on the arm or raised eyebrows. He will also give me hints when he is getting fidgety and needs to change the conversation before he is *'rude'*, as he knows it is socially unacceptable as I have explained it to him but he almost can't help himself.

Communicating important information

"A few of the AS men complained that their partners accused them of not listening, and claimed that their partners will say that they have told them things that they are sure they haven't. Selective hearing is an issue raised by the majority, if not all, of the NT women I spoke to, and seems to be the catalyst for many of the disagreements that evolve between the couples. There is a high level of probability that the NT women have given their AS partners the information, but the AS person does not have any memory of what she has said. The reason is that the information probably never reached long term memory". *Asperger's in Love. Maxine Aston. 2003*

Sometimes I tell Max things and he doesn't remember them, this can be important information, details of doctors appointments or where and when to collect children from school etc, but if I have not had his full attention at the time I am wasting my breath. I have been mid flow and noticed a glazed or unfocussed look on his face so will stop talking and wait until he realises I am still looking at him but not talking. He will ask me what I want to say and I will start again. I often tell him that I have been chatting and he just switched off. We have a chuckle about it and then carry on. I don't think it is the subject matter that causes him to switch off, merely something that has distracted him whether that is a phrase that I have used and he is busy trying to make sense of it, or something on the TV. Max is virtually incapable of doing two things at once as he cannot focus on either and becomes frozen, unable to decide which one to do. He is unable to listen to two conversations or listen if his focus is taken away from the communicator. An example is when he is on the phone and I hear him say something which I feel needs enlarging on or more explanation given, such as a direction to a place, if I try and say "tell them to look out for the..." or other potentially useful information, then he has to ask the person on the phone to wait, turns to me greatly annoyed by my interruption and asks what I want. I will explain what I was trying to say which he will either repeat to the person on the phone, but more likely he will hand the phone to me and suggest if I can do better then I should finish the call myself. This may sound a little odd but he gets very confused and annoyed that he has been interrupted, finding it hard to relay the information between me and the person on the phone once his concentration has been broken. He cannot pass on the information as I am saying it, he has to listen to all the information from me and then try to remember and repeat it on the phone. If it is too much for him he finds it easier to hand the phone to me so I can tell the person directly. Most people are able to hear the information and pass it on as the person is saying it.

Max mulls over things that have been said to him analysing it from every angle, this can be very difficult since I do not have a particularly good memory for incidental information. If I do not feel it is vital to remember the exact details of a conversation or incident then I will push it to the back of my mind. Days, weeks or months later Max will refer to a conversation or incident with perfect clarity as if it had happened that day but I find it very difficult to recall clearly. If he has felt that it was a negative thing, or he has misunderstood the situation surrounding the comment or incident and has escalated it over the period of time, it is very difficult for me to discuss it as I cannot recall exactly what occurred or led up to the conversation. My advice is to try not to say or do anything that can be misinterpreted or misleading, especially about feelings or your relationship. You may be questioned about it sometime later especially if he has put a negative slant on the comment or action and he feels insignificant or criticised. It is very hard, but with good communication, and an understanding of his need to process anything and everything that he doesn't fully understand or takes as a negative comment about him or his behaviour, it is getting easier. Over time he has realised I am not being deliberately nasty, critical or difficult and that he may have misinterpreted something I said or the way in which it was said. I have got used to it and am much better at phrasing things in a less emotional manner, but it does require constant thought.

Max doesn't understand the purpose of small talk. If you don't have something useful, factual or interesting to say then don't say anything. He is far more relaxed with conversations which require known factual answers, a type of 'script' or expected response to a question. Because these are learnt they may occasionally be given as if he is reading them from a book in an almost monotone way. This said; Max is getting better at listening to, and taking part in small talk, in part because he is more able to access the conversation because I can re word or explain anything he misunderstands or mishears. His one liners are amusing and hide any lack of confidence or awkwardness leaving listeners amused and him feeling part of the group. If you have no concept of AS and its effects on day to day communication with peers, work colleagues and family, it is virtually impossible to see how difficult a time a person with AS has on a daily basis. He hides his differences very well, and to the outsider appears to have enjoyed the conversation interacting well, yet in fact he comes away stressed, and in turmoil over all the information that now needs to be processed and translated into a format that he finds easier to understand. Some of the information, in particular the emotional and body language, will go unnoticed so often the information will make no sense at all.

Sometimes, when an AS person is confronted with a comment or perceived criticism, they will respond by saying nothing as they literally do not know what to say and do not wish to ask for clarification on the subject matter, for fear of appearing not to have understood. It is therefore easier to remain silent. This can appear very strange to the people around but it is a safety net for the AS person. I can usually detect these moments and remove us from the situation allowing him to make sense of the information, often with my help, or sometimes when things are obviously too complicated I will move us away from the group so I can explain in private.

G & C Slater Walker talk about arguments they have had.... "Time and time again, I explained that he should either apologise or disagree with me, at least say something, yet he never seemed to do that. Finally, one day, sometime after he had been diagnosed, I asked Chris why he did not say anything, and eventually (there is a long processing time) he explained that he simply did not know what to say.
A further complication was that often Chris was silently feeling he had 'failed' yet again, but because he did not say anything, I did not know that that was the case. This was particularly sad, because that does suggest that he genuinely regretted what he may have done and that was all I wanted to know. My continued nagging must have compounded his feelings of 'getting it wrong' and

51

eventually causing his anger with me. Because he does not understand what I am thinking then he could not resolve the situation by saying something to mollify me. Understanding why he is silent has helped a great deal, but it can still feel frustrating."
An Asperger Marriage. Gisela and Christopher Slater-Walker.

Max is never wrong! I am used to this and usually just let him get away with it. The children find it very difficult to cope with and I cannot explain it is part of his AS, as they do not know he has it, this is because he does not want them to know. I am sure a lot of it is down to his insecurities and not wanting to back down or admit that he might be wrong or not entirely correct. At times it is very frustrating, especially when it is something we have discussed previously and agreed and he has forgotten the conversation, probably because he has been distracted at some point during the initial conversation. If he tells me that we have discussed something and agreed a certain course of action, particularly to do with the children's hectic social life then I will readily accept this. I have no reason to doubt what he is saying as this type of information he has a very keen memory for. This may be because he needs to get a routine sorted out in his head, so has focussed hard on the conversation and remembered the agreed details. It is then set in stone and cannot be changed. This can prove slightly difficult when the children throw in changes as children are prone to do. These can be simple things such as wanting to bring a friend along or not returning from school at the normal time. We can get round this but it unsettles Max and he will keep reminding everyone that this was not the original plan.

Max also has to be the best at everything or be the sickest! If one of the children is poorly then he will list all his illnesses as if he doesn't want to be outdone. He finds it really hard to show sympathy he will cuddle them if they sit on him and 'demand' it, but he would not volunteer it though he has some understanding of their need to be 'cuddled better'.

Max asks me to explain things he sees going on around him. He watches couples, groups etc in great detail, in fact, he often gets so transfixed by the situation he will stop in his tracks and stare open mouthed at them. It is often so obvious that I try and distract him, as I am terrified that one of these days someone will take offence and get nasty. He doesn't mean to stare he just becomes fascinated and totally engrossed in the scene that is playing out in front of him, blanking everything else around him. It is very difficult if not impossible for an AS person to focus on more than one thing at a time. Once the scene has played out, or I have successfully distracted him, he will ask me to explain why certain people were acting in a particular way, why when one person said 'x' the other person reacted as they did. He wants to know why something had elicited a seemingly violent, sad or happy reaction. I am using descriptions of emotions, however, often he has misinterpreted the reaction and this has confused the scenario even more in his head. What is also interesting and sad is that I can assess what is going on after hearing only a couple of sentences or glancing at the body language as I walk past. I can make judgements using a wide range of social and emotional skills built up over the years. I read the body language, tone of voice, facial expressions; the unsaid information that forms a large proportion of human interaction. As mentioned earlier by Maxine Aston 70% of human communication is unspoken leaving only 30% for the Asperger partner to use, if they are not actively involved in conversation or close enough to pick up the information verbally they stand very little chance of understanding anything. Max does not have this ability to correctly read body language and emotions and never will. This is something that really frustrates him as it doesn't seem fair. I think that the frustration has increased since we became a couple because he socialises far more. We go into town or out and about, we wander and enjoy having coffee in cafes or sitting in parks, before I came along Max would go out, get his shopping and go home. Interestingly I have discovered that there are occasions when I find it very difficult to explain a situation to Max. It is very hard to explain certain types of human interaction to someone who has no understanding of basic emotions. I find it hard to verbalise what you almost instinctively know or understand when put on the spot. I try and explain it using references to situations he might have encountered at work or university. Sometimes it takes a long time and a lot of going over old ground. He is getting a lot better and often reads simple situations fairly accurately, however he does not understand them emotionally. When I asked him why he was so fascinated he said, "*It is something that in my opinion is different and it catches my eye and fascinates me*". He goes on to say, "*My life is a collection of other people's. Our relationship allows me to explore elements of humans but it also highlights my inadequacies. I never went out before, it's exciting, it allows me to enjoy watching people interacting but I always know you are there to rescue me if things get out of hand. Because I am putting myself in these positions it is highlighting my differences. I want to be the same as everyone else but I can't get to be like everyone else*".

One interesting incident that demonstrates his differences and lack of understanding of social etiquette happened early on in our relationship. We had gone to Bournemouth for a weekend break. After a great meal we looked for a nightclub that looked fun and eventually we discovered one that was playing great music. We entered to find that its décor was Egyptian in style even down to the shish pipes, low round padded seats and freshly cooked North African food. It was perfect, the ages of the clientele was varied which offered an interesting mix of conversations. We settled down to chatting to the regulars, having a few drinks naturally gravitating to the dance floor which was quite quiet at that time. We stood watching a young lady dancing seductively in front of her partner, an older man sitting at the bar. Max was fascinated and staring which hadn't gone unnoticed by the man, then he turned to me and said look at the way she dances its very sexy, I agreed but he persisted and started pointing at her telling me why certain moves looked so good. I could see her partner becoming more and more agitated and managed to stop Max from continuing to point, suggesting that he just describe it and not make his interest so obvious. He had no cognition of the partner's annoyance and the potentially volatile situation he was placing himself in, all he wanted to do was point out what a good and sensual dancer the lady was. He was impressed and fascinated by her and obviously hoped I could learn from her, he says I do not dance well and my rhythm is wrong. What he actually means is that it doesn't fit with his view of the perfect dancing partner. Once distracted he suggested that we dance, I readily joined him never for one second thinking I was going to have a very public dancing lesson! We started to dance and soon he was telling me that I should try and dance more slowly, then he started to try and spin me round telling me to focus on a group of lights in one corner of the dance floor, saying that they looked lovely if you span fast as they made really pretty patterns. Try as I might I could not do it to his satisfaction and he kept making me try again. Luckily for both of us and our long term prospects I am not particularly shy, and although I was aware that most of the people nearby and on the dance floor were watching us, I persisted as I knew it was important to him. We spent quite a long time dancing but as the dance floor filled up we decided to move onto the terrace and spent the next hour chatting about Max's Asperger's and how he felt about it. It was still early days so I was better informed than he was and this understanding helped him greatly; he could describe things that had happened in the past and I could explain why he had reacted in a particular way, and why other people had reacted the way they had. It was the start of our learning curve and at this point he had no idea that I had been reading up on Asperger's Syndrome. He was feeling relaxed and at long last understood more about his condition. He was comfortable in my company and our surroundings, this feeling suddenly manifested itself in him deciding to lead me back to the edge of the dance floor where I sat down, Tom Jones was playing and Max proceeded to stand in front of me gyrating his pelvis in a very provocative manner then turned around and wiggled his bottom. This continued throughout the song much to the amazement of those around us. I sat there totally amazed and amused in a slightly embarrassed way but knew he was dancing for me. Max was completely oblivious of those around him and had totally focussed on me and the music and his dance was brilliant. When the music changed he came over and we danced together again. I could not believe what had just happened but over the years there have been repeat performances which I now view with delight, as I know that he is completely happy and relaxed and this guarantees a fabulous evening. I do not care what people around us think as life is far too short to worry about them, we are not hurting anyone else and are happy now. I will frequently play the lead by dancing for him enticing him onto the dance floor which he thoroughly enjoys.

Tone of voice.

Max is quite good at changing his tone of voice to fit the desired mood he thinks he should be portraying, although I think a lot of this has been learnt relatively recently. However, he is bad at recognising the meaning of changes in tone when others are talking. He hears the difference but finds it hard to attach the correct emotion to the tone. I have often said something as a joke and he has taken it as a serious comment and been upset. He misses the inflections which change it from serious to joke. This can cause problems when we are socialising especially if someone makes a comment as a joke and Max thinks they are serious. I usually have to make it very obvious to Max that it was said as a joke before he responds seriously and embarrasses himself.

Social conventions

Max doesn't understand the usual social conventions. He is childlike in his outlook and so tends to want to do 'childish things'; although I dare say that if people were not so concerned about what strangers thought of them, we would all be a little more childlike and enjoy life more. It is fun to be silly sometimes but so often society prohibits these sudden desires from being pursued. He felt the need to go up an escalator the wrong way one day and asked if it was ok. When I said it was fine he took great delight in having been 'allowed' and spent several minutes playing much to the amazement of the people around us. I received a few strange glances as if I should stop him but he was enjoying himself and wasn't hurting anyone else. Another time he wanted to learn to use inline rollerblades.

After spending a great deal of time on the internet finding us both a pair we went to a large, very public open area, and spent several hours trying to stay upright. Needless to say Max mastered it very quickly, I am sure this was because, like a child, he had no fear of falling over or being watched or judged. I, on the other hand, was very conscious that I could break bones and that many people both young and old were watching intently fascinated by our activities, after a while people who passed by commented on how brave we were and how well we were doing. It was as if they would have loved to have been able to try it, but didn't have the nerve. When we are in the supermarket Max will gradually pick up speed with the trolley and then lift his feet off the ground and let the trolley whiz down the aisle, he loves it and all the more because 'I allow' him to do it.

"Supermarkets seem to be one of the few places where AS men feel they can behave like children again and a few have been known to take a ride on a trolley, whizzing up and down the aisles completely oblivious to the shoppers around them". Maxine Aston Asperger's in Love 2003

It has been quite liberating for me too. During my first marriage I changed from a vibrant, outgoing, risk taking biker into a mouse as a result of physical and mental abuse. My second marriage allowed me to regain some semblance of my former self. Having children ensured I became a responsible mother. Being with Max has certainly added a lot of colour to my life, there is never a dull moment and regressing to my childhood thoughts and pursuits has certainly been great fun and very stimulating. It is OK to have fun although our motivations are different; Max knows that certain age groups are expected to behave in particular ways from learnt and observed behaviour, however, he gets sudden urges to do things that

58

don't fit with expected adult behaviour. In the past he would suppress the urge to do it as he knew the response from others might not be positive, now he knows that I don't mind him doing it and this makes him feel safe. He knows that I will stop him if he goes a little too far. I have always admired people who do eccentric things and I used to when I was younger, but haven't got the confidence anymore but, by allowing Max to enjoy himself and seeing how much fun he gets from such simple things, I am getting braver and we have so much fun; such as on one occasion we spontaneously started dancing in a large shop in Southampton to a tune we particularly liked, this certainly raised some eyebrows but also a lot of smiles, next time we will go for applause! He also does an excellent impression of Noel Coward which he frequently uses in 'posh' restaurants, such a laugh but difficult to keep up for any length of time, so it totally confuses those people listening. I would recommend it to everyone, try to step out of that social comfort zone once in a while and enjoy life, people aren't as critical as you might think and anyway you only live once so make the most of it. Now I am much more inclined to initiate something silly as I know he will not judge me.

"We are very playful and happy; generally laughing and messing about. We have a lot of motivation to do nice things together...I remember once when in a shopping centre and upon seeing the escalators Keith said that he had always wondered what it would be like to run up the down escalator. I said 'Go on then', so off he ran and flung himself up the escalator, almost wrenching his arm out of its socket in the process. He seemed gleeful that he had been given permission to do what he had always pondered. In this, I suppose we are partners in crime as I clearly have little regard for social approval and actively encourage his quirkiness and individuality". Keith says,

"With regard to the escalator and similar urges that I have; I know that some of the things I want to do, but shouldn't because I have a sense aren't socially acceptable, suddenly become available to me when encouraged (or at least not discouraged) by Sarah and take on a sense of possibility because she is in the real world. Therefore if she can behave in such a way, it must be OK for me to do so, and my previous misgivings must have been wrong. I understand that Sarah is not strongly bound by petty rules or boundaries, yet is still non-AS and socially included".

I completely agree with Sarah and think it is the childlike quality in all of us that is brought out by the AS partner. Although I was not as confident as Sarah obviously is, when Max and I first met, mainly due to my previous relationships, like her I have never had much interest or regard for social conventions trying to be myself, I used to wear a 'Mary Poppins' style hat, much to my children's horror, because it made me feel happy. Max has allowed me to get back to the more carefree approach to life that I had before the disastrous marriages. By 'allowing' Max to do these fun things I free myself up and can enjoy them as well. I do think that you have to be a certain type of person if the relationship is to succeed, as you will find it very hard to relax in social settings, if you are unable to ignore people's looks and comments when you partner says or does something not quite 'acceptable', then I do not think that the relationship will last. It does get easier when you relax; I take the view that as long as no one is hurt by what you are doing and it doesn't damage property, then life is too short to worry about narrow minded individuals who are missing out on great amounts of fun, by not allowing themselves to step outside social convention occasionally. In this day and age of thrill seeking at great expense, more people should try simple things like dancing in a supermarket, it's a lot cheaper and great fun, it even brings a smile to other people's faces.

Max functions best in social situations when there is an element of control, that's me, as he knows that I will save him from awkward situations. I don't have to stay at his side all the time, but do watch his expressions and body language closely so I can get him out of trouble if necessary. Although Max is probably not conscious of this it allows him to experiment with social interactions, if you like, I am his fail safe as well as his protector.

Self-gratification.

Max has no stop signals. When we go out to a night club he has to stay to the bitter end, if they are still serving drinks at the bar he will have another one even if he is quite drunk. If I try to stop him he will pout, in a childlike manner and imply that I am spoiling the evening. Once out of the club he will then follow the routine and go to the chip shop where he will order far too much and try and eat it on the way home. He can't or won't see that we have had a great night but it is time to go home. It is far more enjoyable walking home together chatting on the way than trying to drag a staggering man home. When we get home I usually feel like going to bed, it is around 0400, but he will say *"oh not yet"*, so I stay up to keep him company. I am not very good company because I am so tired, and he will comment on this asking why I am quiet or unhappy. Often when he has eaten or drunk too much and we go to bed I will lie next to him with my back to him and he will gently turn me over by touching my side and tugging. Once I am on my side facing him, he will take my hand and place it on his tummy. I know this is so I can rub it in a rhythmical circular motion. He will say *"Annie, I don't feel well"* I say *"I know"* and will rub his tummy for 20

61

minutes or until he goes to sleep. I don't mind doing this because it helps him to relax but it is quite one sided. I know that if he hadn't eaten or drunk so much he would not be feeling so poorly, but he just can't stop, even with my best efforts to dissuade him there is no stop button once he sets his mind to something. The same applies if I have cooked something he particularly likes and there is some leftover, he will eat it even if he is not hungry and then regrets it, feeling bloated and uncomfortable. There are several other things that he finds impossible to eat in moderation, chocolate and sweets being the main offenders.

Chapter 9

Obsessions

It is perfectly normal for the AS person to be obsessive. With Max the obsessions vary, with an overriding interest in all things technical; goods such as cameras, ipods, speakers, power tools, usually bought for one job and rarely used again, in fact the list is diverse and yet the same attention to detail in the search applies equally to each and every item. Once he has focussed on a particular item he will spend hours on the internet researching in minute detail specifications and technical information, comparing all of it and looking for the best possible item. Price has a degree of importance but it is not the main focus. Once the item with the best specifications has been identified, he will trawl the internet to find the best price. Financially we are limited, however, once the vital item has been located he will then keep mentioning it to me at every opportunity. It would be much easier to say, "Yes buy it", but financially it often stretches the budget. It is a childlike need on which he becomes totally focused and he just has to have it, and all the typical AS logical reasoning goes out of the window. Once the new 'toy' has been acquired, all the information he has worked so hard to find over the months and quoted in great detail, is no longer required so it is erased from his mind; it is not necessary and of no consequence. He will move on to the next obsession and it will start again, this may not be an immediate move and there may be a few months grace but be assured there will be another item which is vital! Be prepared to become an internet widow!

Max has a passion for all things shiny, *"Out of school I always had a passion for picking up shiny things or interesting things. I was constantly searching, walking around with my head in the kerb. I liked things that didn't fit into their surroundings; my pockets were always full of bits of metal, marbles, bottle caps etc. The most memorable thing I ever picked up was a thing that looked like a magnifying glass, a small loop of metal, without the glass. As I got older I looked on tips and in skips, it was an absolute pleasure searching for things that were different. I spent an enormous amount of time on a landfill site not looking for anything in particular just unusual stuff. I kept it all in a large stiff old fashioned suitcase under my bed".*

This collection moved where ever he went and nearly got him into a lot of trouble. He had been working at an old ladies house fitting draft exclusion equipment and had a visit from the police. The woman had accused him of stealing a ring. The police searched his house and discovered his suitcase of 'found' stuff. In amongst the treasures were a number of ring boxes which obviously, under the circumstances, looked suspicious; Max was quite embarrassed as the police were obviously amazed and confused as to why anyone would want to keep such a collection of seemingly useless things. The old lady found the ring and Max was no longer implicated, however, after the traumatic experience and violation of his privacy he took the suitcase to the dump. Even today he still looks for and picks things up as we are out and about, things which catch his eye and fascinate him, he spots them from a distance and just has to pick them up. They are usually shiny things as this has caught his eye in the first place.

"There is an intense interest in collecting these items at every opportunity. The child appears to have a visual acuity that identifies each specimen from some distance and cannot be distracted or persuaded to abandon an opportunity to collect just one more....There appears to be a developmental sequence in the nature of the interests,

64

and the next stage is a fascination with a topic rather than an object". Tony Attwood. Asperger's Syndrome. A guide for parents and Professionals.

His love of things shiny has led to a vast knowledge of the quality of diamonds, precious stones and gold. Not long after I started to see him he showed me his collection of jewellery. It was very impressive and had been purchased over the internet over a long period of time. He had saved information from the original purchase and knew so much about each piece, far more than the seller had posted in the original advert. He could tell me the quality of each diamond and had lots of equipment used to test the quality of gold and diamonds. I was fascinated and very impressed especially since I love pretty rings. He has used this knowledge to great effect on several occasions. We have gone into jewellers to look at eternity and engagement rings and also to help friends buy similar rings. He has been shown a variety of rings often over priced for the quality. Max has asked for an eye glass which has surprised the jeweller and then proceeded to discuss the quality of the stone, saying that it has a slight occlusion, a technical term, or other equally knowledgeable information. As a result he has had a discount or been offered a much better quality product. The large collection of rings proved very useful when we decided to get married, as the local jeweller took them in as almost full payment for a spectacular pair of wedding rings.

Bathroom stuff.

Max likes his bathroom things in the right place, likes to see the labels on products facing forward and all the tops must be shut on the bottles. To Max this seems a logical way to place things and gives him a sense of order. I am not the most ordered person in the world and most of our rooms, for Max, are nightmare, but in his own small way in the bathroom, he can still have some order in our rather small chaotic home.

Max is very particular about his personal hygiene, the cleanliness of the bathroom and in particular the toilet. He likes to clean the bathroom and so I leave it to him. He has a very specific way of doing it, everything is removed then the bath, toilet, sink, shower and shelves are cleaned with copious amounts of strong anti-bacterial cleaner. Then the floor, this becomes a virtual swimming pool of strong smelling cleaner, pushed around with a mop until all areas are well and truly covered. He leaves it for ten minutes to kill the germs then mops it all up. He has ruined several pairs of trousers where he splashes the cleaning fluid so energetically, but it has to be done!

Max is very specific when it comes to shoes. Several years ago he decided that he wanted a particular style of shoes, this was not because of something he had seen it was an idea he had decided would be the ultimate in comfort. No-one made anything like it at that time. Eventually a company called 'Art' made a shoe that fitted his remit. Now these are the only shoes he will wear. They come in a wide range of colours so, when we decided to get married, we went searching for Art shoes in the theme colour for the wedding, burgundy. To his delight we were successful and he wore them on the big day. I was very happy with his choice as I knew they were exactly what he wanted and he would be much more comfortable. The interesting thing was that many of the guests were horrified, as they thought he should have worn formal black shoes, they couldn't understand that I was happy with his choice and pleased that Max was comfortable.

Chapter 10

Emotions

"People with AS are not generally emotionless - it is emotional understanding that often cause problems, rather than a lack of emotions themselves". Asperger Syndrome & Social Relationships Genevieve Edmonds and Luke Beardon.

Max describes emotion in a very practical way; he likens it to an electrical circuit where a piece has worked loose. At the start of our relationship the wiring wasn't too bad and there were more demonstrations of 'emotion' but as time has progressed and the stress levels have risen, the wiring has become disconnected again with only the occasional spark.

It is really hard to form a relationship when someone does not show any emotion and has no empathy with your emotional needs. It is emotionally draining and a great strain on the relationship.

I understand that he finds it very difficult to respond when I am emotional; but I find it incredibly hard to deal with. I don't try to get a response because he gets frustrated, a bit like a child who doesn't understand. I bottle it up usually, because, when I am feeling down, I do not feel able to discuss my feelings rationally. It is hard to cope when all you want is a cuddle and a few reassuring words, and your partner does not have the ability to give you this. In the early days I often cried myself to sleep. I still do occasionally, but this is more me feeling sorry for myself and expecting too much of Max. The problem is that in many ways he can often recognise when I am troubled, and will now try to make the right noises, but because of this I then expect more and when it doesn't happen I get upset. Again I do not discuss it until I am less emotional. I have to time this, because if Max is stressed or under pressure, he does not want or need to try and listen to or talk about emotions that he doesn't understand, or how I would have liked him to react. If my timing is wrong the comments can be perceived as a criticism or failure on his part. I find it hard when he turns his back on me if I say something that he doesn't want to hear, or he takes something I have said the wrong way and won't let me explain what I actually meant by the comment. He is always joking and teasing and this is fun, he enjoys it when I play along. However, if I start it and he doesn't realise or 'get it' then he turns his back. The incident will be brought up days later and I will try to clarify what I said but even then it doesn't always clear the air. An example was one evening whilst we were chatting in bed I said "You really are the most pampered man" he replied "*I pamper you!*" and I said "Yeah right", he instantly turned his back and said he was very hurt. I had wanted to tease him and say I should be living in a palace etc but wasn't able to continue the conversation. Three days later he reminded me and said he was very hurt. I told him that if he had allowed me to continue I would have explained that I needed a palace and fineries. He still maintains that is not what I meant which is hurtful. In fact I often tell him how pampered I feel, showered with unexpected gifts such as flowers for no reason other than he thought I would like them, little gifts of chocolates and many more yet he still will not accept that I was playing. So as a word of warning be careful what you say even in jest. It is not that Max doesn't love me because I know he does, this is demonstrated in hundreds of ways but when I get into bed I often feel lonely. We cuddle for a few minutes, this is because I told him that is what I wanted each night and then he rolls over and goes to sleep. There are times when

I really need him to just hold me while I cry and talk irrationally about a situation. I don't expect a solution as such, but I would like someone to say 'don't worry' or 'it will be fine in the morning' - just make the right noises.

He hates it if I get a cold because when I sniff he thinks I am crying. One day he told me that it had taken him ages to pluck up the courage to ask what was wrong, and was very relieved when I told him I had a cold and wasn't crying or upset.

Over time I have began to understand better and am not as upset plus our very in depth and soul searching conversations have helped greatly. These have helped Max to respond to some of my emotional needs, this is learnt behaviour and not an empathetic reaction but it is still appreciated and I don't think about the lack of emotional content, as I know that if Max could 'do' emotion then he would. It is a constant source of frustration to him and me. He would love to feel the emotions that I do, sometimes I get what he calls, 'a flowery moment', he knows I am having a flowery moment because I cuddle up next to him, squeeze him tightly and give him a kiss on the cheek whilst making a little squeal of delight. When this first happened he said, "*What was that all about?*" I told him that I had just felt a sudden urge to hug and cuddle him because I was feeling so happy and close to him, everything at that precise moment was perfect, like a beautiful garden filled with flowers and freshly mown grass on a hot summer's day. This was an analogy he could understand and visualise saying, "*I have smelt those memories*", he thought it was weird, but over time he got used to it and in some ways understands how I am feeling. Now when I am really happy about something he uses the term 'flowery' to describe how I am feeling and says, "*You are feeling flowery aren't you?*" The description of the emotion has helped Max understand how I am feeling which helps, but at the same time he wishes that he could have these emotions which sound so nice, so there has been a negative side to it as well. On balance Max likes to have a visual description of an emotion as it helps him to start to understand it.

"Simon talks about his visual thinking.' When I think, it is mainly using "pictures" and I find it hard to think with words. In my mind I can play short movies almost at will. Until I became an adult I didn't even realise that many other people don't actually think this way. The other day, I asked one of my friends to use their memory to picture a dog. If I think of a dog in my mind I can see lots of movie clips with the dog doing different activities. I can even change the colour of the dog's fur or make the dog run backwards". Asperger Syndrome in Adults. Dr Ruth Searle 2010

Max feels very guilty over his 'lack' of emotional understanding saying,

"I naturally default to the easy option, the one which springs to mind first. Emotions are a bit like this, I don't get them but know they exist, and I know I should feel them and that you (Annie) need me to feel them, which is where the guilt comes in. Guilt is an emotion, I am not devoid of emotions, but they are skewed and I feel guilty that I don't default to the normal emotional response to a situation. I may not have experienced them but I do know they exist, I think that the strongest 'normal' response I have had is when I have inadvertently upset a child through something I have said, I probably would not know what the actual word or sentence was that had upset them but I would know I had done it. It would really upset me because upsetting a child is the last thing I want to do, kids are not as complex as adults and I think I can read

their emotions better as they are not as confusing as those of adults. My dilemma is that I feel my own emotions but I can't feel or understand other people's emotions. I know they have them it's like a rumour, I detect something but I just can't get it! If someone hurt me I would have an emotional response to it, but if someone hurt you (Annie) I would know you were hurt, you would tell me but I couldn't feel it with you. I can't empathise with you. I can't see it, feel it or get it, but intellectually I know you are experiencing something, but I just can't work out exactly what it is and I hate myself for that because you need me to understand."

Displays of emotion

Max was at university when his mum died, she had been ill for some time. When his sister phoned him to say she was dead Max just thought *"dead, not here, not existing?"* It was difficult to cope with why she was dead because she wasn't there anymore, *"didn't exist"*. After the conversation Max went to his room at the university and just cried. He found it hard to explain this action and said, *"Crying is an emotion but in true honesty I cried because I thought that is what I should do, isn't that awful. I cried for half an hour. After getting over the understanding that she wasn't going to be here anymore, I went to the funeral and that sort of thing, then I got on with my course".*

"One of the features of Asperger's syndrome...is a tendency to laugh or giggle in circumstances when one would anticipate an expression of embarrassment, discomfort, pain or sadness. There have been instances of grief over the death of a member of the family being expressed by laughter or mania (Berthier 1995) or even indifference. This is due to the inability to express appropriate and subtle emotions. Asperger's Syndrome. A

71

Guide for Parents and Professionals. Tony Attwood 1998
Max says, "*Humans can be quite predictable so I can predict reactions but I do not understand it. It is a bit like a+b=c, I can understand that 2+2=4 I have accepted this and can regurgitate it but do not understand it*".

"*If I am feeling sad and someone else is feeling sad with me I can get it because I understand it from my perspective*".

One evening at cadets Max was called into the 1st Lieutenant's office, was accused of making one of the older cadets cry and was given a dressing down. He was very upset about this as he was not aware that he had. He went to see the commanding officer to complain and asked him to investigate. After much investigating Max was vindicated and received an apology.

"*I have great difficulty registering emotions. A girl cried at cadets one evening and I didn't get it. I saw the tears but didn't register it as an emotion and that something had happened to make her cry. It's something I cannot describe something I do not understand. I know this happened but I didn't get it, the emotion, so didn't do anything about it. The commanding officer said, that I didn't do anything wrong except you just didn't recognise it and I realised he was right.*"

Max is a very caring and generous man. He knows I like flowers so buys them often and for no reason. The first time he bought them, beautiful pink roses, he came home puzzled. He told me that when he had got to the checkout the cashier had looked at him in a 'knowing' way and asked him what he had done wrong. He was very puzzled and replied, "*Nothing*", she was surprised and informed him that most men only buy flowers when they have either done something wrong as a peace offering, or they are about to do something that their partner will be unhappy about, such as go out for an evening with the lads and it is a way to soften the blow. He was intrigued and asked me to explain what she had meant and was it really true. I explained that from my own past experiences and from chatting to friends, this was a fairly accurate interpretation of the male act of taking flowers home, and it didn't have to be flowers you could add chocolates to the list. He was amazed and couldn't understand why men would do this, *"why not just apologise or not upset the partner in the first place, and why did people feel they couldn't go out for an evening with friends"*. He added he wouldn't want to go out without me.

When I get flowers it is because he has been thinking about me, they are chosen with care, thought and 'love', well I call it that! He selects the colours and types I like best, and the ones with the longest 'best before' date so I can enjoy them longer. They are not just any bunch grabbed from a bucket in a petrol station on the way home from work, they have meaning and emotion for me even if he doesn't feel or understand it.

I started saving the petals from each bunch and pressing them. He really could not grasp the concept of wanting to preserve a few petals from a flower that was about to die and could be replaced. I tried to explain that I wanted to preserve each moment and this was partly because, for the majority of my life, I only got bought flowers for the very reasons implied by the cashier, and not because anyone was genuinely thinking about me and how much I would appreciate the gesture. I hope one day to make a beautiful collage rather like a timeline of flowers; it's the artist in me as well as my sentimental side.

Pink toilet block! Fancy that I didn't know it existed yet he found it. This was Max's way of showing that he loved me, wanted me to be happy and cheer up. What you have to understand is that the AS partner finds it hard to understand why we are down, and can't identify with our emotional needs. Max's way of showing me that he was thinking of me and trying to empathise with me was his gift of a pink toilet block. I will explain, I had worked a night shift, slept for four hours and then gone to the dentists. I have a real phobia about the dentist; shaking, crying and general irrational behaviour. Just before I was due to go in I received a phone call telling me that my job application had not been successful which, rather than a quick "I am sorry" was a lengthy explanation of why I was not successful. The dental treatment was terrible and I ended up nearly fainting at the receptionist's desk as I was leaving the surgery, much to her horror! Once home I didn't tell Max, as I didn't want to do it in front of the children and was going to wait until they had gone out to cadets. I opened a package which had arrived whilst I slept only to discover that it was our IVA [Individual Voluntary Agreement] plan, it showed that financially we were in real trouble and would be living hand to mouth for the next five years. I felt totally flat and emotionally exhausted, but knew that I had to stay jolly and not show the turmoil inside. Once the children had gone out I decided to have a lie down and recharge my batteries. Max came in and I decided to tell him about the job but ended up explaining how I felt at the dentist and then discussed the IVA plan. He couldn't or wouldn't see that, the more I earnt the more we paid to the IVA, so it didn't help if I worked more hours we would still lose the money. All I wanted to do was cry but I couldn't do it in front of Max as he cannot deal with me being down, let alone crying. If I show this facially he gets very worried and confused. I went and sat in the living room and started to have a good cry, soon after Max appeared and asked if I had been crying. I said yes and left it at that, he suggested we go shopping for food. I agreed and en route he asked very factually not emotionally why I was "*so depressed*". I told him I wasn't depressed just tired, had had a terrible day and was cold. He replied that he had two of the three things; he was tired and had had a bad day. He could not accept or understand that I might be feeling flatter at that specific moment than he was, and needed a few minutes of emotional pampering and restoration through words or cuddling. We shopped and once home he presented me with the pink toilet block, pink is my favourite colour. It was his way of showing me that he was trying to support me. I love the toilet block its great so girly, no man would normally allow it in their house. This was his way of showing me that he wanted me to feel better.

This is something that I think any non AS partner must acknowledge and accept for their relationship to work. They cannot do the emotional communication in the same way that we do or expect. If you are open to this you will notice that in their way they make up for it, just allow them time, and explain what you would like when you feel a little down. Just be prepared for the unexpected; in fact a toilet block as a present would mean more to Max than smelly toiletries like shower gel as he is very sensitive to many products, so a practical gift is far more acceptable. When Max read this he considered it for a moment and said "*I'm showing you in pink*". He had made an effort to personalise the gift by choosing my favourite colour, pink.

Max, despite his belief that he is 'cold' is fantastic at choosing cards and presents. He puts thought and consideration into them producing wonderfully appropriate sentimental gifts. Our first Christmas together, I received two very expensive necklaces, diamonds and sapphires set in 18ct gold, many little fun and practical gifts and a card with beautiful words both printed and hand written. Interestingly the necklaces nearly caused an incident. He had spent months researching and sourcing them both, they had to be specifically styled and he had decided when he was going to give them to me, based on the dresses I had intended to wear for the Christmas Eve and Christmas Day. I was oblivious to this thought process so, after my bath, I started to get ready to go out, Max talked about which dress I intended to wear that night and I replied "the pink one" I proceeded to change while he had a bath. When he emerged from the bathroom I was dressed, in the wrong dress! This was his perception, as far as I was concerned the dress I was wearing was pink and the other dress was cerise and black. He said *"why are you wearing that dress?"* and I replied "this is my pink one". He was obviously upset and so I offered to change after discovering that he had thought I was wearing the cerise one. He was flustered and told me not to bother it would be ok and he would change his plans. I really had no idea what the problem was until he handed me two jewellery boxes and explained that he had wanted to give me the trilogy diamond necklace on Christmas Eve to wear with the cerise dress and the diamond and sapphire necklace on Christmas Day with the pink dress. I had completely thrown him and he felt that I had to have both because he couldn't alter his plans for the order that the necklaces were given in. I was completely overwhelmed and much to his bemusement started to cry. He thought he had upset me until I explained that I was crying because I had never been treated so well and the sentiment of the trilogy, I love you, was so powerful and something I never thought would have been demonstrated by him. He brushed this comment aside and it took another 18 months for him to actually say the words, and then they were quantified by the fact that if love means wanting to care for someone completely and without condition then he must love me! His problem with the words, I love you, was that he had no concept of what love was. He had seen so many varying and conflicting examples on TV and in films, most of which usually ended in tragedy or divorce, that he had little positive influences to go on particularly since he is not a fan of what he calls, "*girly films*". The words "I love you" are important to me and once Max realised I needed to hear them he made a supreme effort to say them more often. The frequency increases when he has had a couple of drinks and his guard is down. I respond with, "I love you too" and he will add, "*No I really do love you*". I love it when he says it, and I genuinely think that he does feel some emotional concept when he says it although it is his interpretation of love, that is, there is no-one else in the world he wants to spend the rest of his life with or understands him as I do.

On Christmas day I opened many more gifts all beautifully wrapped and very personal, a little book called Purple Ronnie's little guide to boyfriends particularly springs to mind, but all of them showed time and effort spent trawling round shops and on the internet to find presents that I would enjoy. Some would argue that this is learnt behaviour yet how can one learn about someone's character, likes and dislikes, if you don't take time and effort listening and observing; that in itself demonstrated interest and affection. Many men, and in particular the ones I have been associated with in the past, have put very little if any thought into presents, two I received spring to mind, a wheelbarrow and a set of saucepans hardly demonstrated love and a personal touch, more a desperate last minute attempt to find something to wrap up. Max continues to shower me with presents on special occasions making me feel wonderful and much loved. He treats me like a Lady and in fact thanks to him I am one! A couple of Christmas's ago I found in my Christmas sack a document saying that I owned part of an estate in Scotland which entitled the owner to the title of Lady. He had purchased the land because he thought I should have a title, such chivalry, my knight in shining armour. He is a perfect gentleman something his Mum had instilled in him many years ago. He carries heavy bags joking that it is a man thing and never allows anyone to be rude to me. This was a major issue when the children moved in with us and the older ones visited. As far as he was concerned his upbringing had taught him that no-one should disrespect their mother. He would never have dreamed of speaking to his Irish Mum the way my children spoke to me, and he felt that I did far too much for them often without a word of thanks. He had grown up in a family of 9 being the second oldest. Their father had left when Max was quite young and as the second eldest, Max had done a lot of the caring. All the children had chores and treated their Mum with the utmost respect.

Over the years I think I had found it easier not to get into confrontation with my 5 children, and felt quite badly about the fact their father had been of little support and influence during their formative years; he would sit in the living room whilst I struggled to keep the peace, cook the tea and sort out the children's social calendars without the slightest hint of interest or offer of help. I had played both disciplinarian and carer often with the lines blurring and leaving me exhausted from constantly feeling inadequate. When he left I felt a sense of guilt and fear. We should have split up years before, but I didn't think I could provide adequately well for the children alone, with hind sight I can see that I could have and would have done just fine. Three of the boys blamed me totally for the separation having listened to their father's version of events. Max found their disrespect appalling, and immediately set about insisting that they treated me with the respect he said I deserved. Gradually they have changed the way they speak to me, now they would never dream of taking me for granted, as Max will pick them up on that immediately. Even little things such as please and thank you, which I value so much yet were often lacking, are common place now, they help with dishes and cooking and do not touch things which do not belong to them without asking permission first. It has completely changed our relationship and I am very grateful to Max for this. His insistence and persistence has certainly made a huge difference to the way our family functions and interacts.

Just as Max demands respect and appreciation of me from the children, it is very apparent that he appreciates everything that I do for him. Simple things, such as making a cup of coffee, cooking supper or ironing his work shirts illicit a heartfelt thank you. These things are so simple and I enjoy doing them for him yet many are taken for granted by partners, husbands, wives and families regarded as expected or even unnoticed. Max regards them as special and worthy of acknowledgement. It is amazing how strange that felt for me, I guess I hadn't appreciated how undervalued and taken for granted I had been for so many years. At first I thought he was just being polite which was very nice but I didn't expect the 'on best behaviour' bit to last but it has and I love it. The children see him treating me with respect and appreciation and they are learning, with help from him in the form of constant reminders and demonstration, that common courtesies cost nothing yet are so appreciated.

Chapter 11

Max as a Step Dad

Max really works at being a good Dad. He has put in place routines for the children such as; they must change their school clothes as soon as they get home. They have set bed times and pocket money is earnt. He is very good at playing with both the younger children and the two eldest chat to him as a "male" role model someone who will put a man's slant on their worldly problems. They also appreciate the fact that he makes me very happy. I am a very different person from the one they remember from several years ago. The middle child has still to form a strong bond with Max and I know this grates a little with him. He desperately wants both the younger children to call him Dad. Our little girl, Charlotte, is very loving towards him and readily calls him Dad but our teenager is still resistant to the idea, he feels it is disrespectful to his biological dad. I do try and explain to Max that in every other way he is regarded as Dad, by our son; Patrick cuddles him all the time and they have wonderful play fights and games on the Xbox. Max in return treats him more affectionately than his biological dad does so it is incredibly difficult for both of them. Patrick is aware that Max would like him to call him Dad, although he does not tell him just me. He has slipped up a few times but I think it will be a long haul, one which Max finds increasingly difficult as he is giving so much of himself and feels it is such a small thing to do for our son. He says "*I want him to call me Dad and when he doesn't it causes me trauma. Words are more important than actions he can hug me 1000 times but the word means more, it is important, I need the confirmation, I need to know and he has never done that. The only slight comfort I get is when you refer to me as Dad and he doesn't dispute it*".

Another conversation we had about the younger children went like this.

Max. "*We have a duty to the children*".

Annie. "Why, what do you mean?"

Max. "*Because they are children and that is the way it is, that is the rule. Don't ask me this complicated question. Charlotte is a child I have a duty to her because of her mental state. I don't want to give it; I just know it is the rule. Here is the dilemma, I give total trust I do what I believe is the moralistic rule. I give it and I expect it back. Kids are more likely to give it back than adults although they are completely strange. When they demand it I give it back. I get totally confused when you tell me that Patrick really loves me. I don't see it, I need something more concrete and 'Dad' is more concrete. Those are the rules if he calls me Dad that is concrete affirmation. When I get called Max that is just what friends say. It doesn't work within the structure*".

Annie. "No I understand completely what you are saying".

Max. "*There you are its completely logical like DATA*".

Max views the behaviour of fathers he meets as bizarre and not how a father should be. His work means that he meets a large cross section of the public and frequently sees men with their children. "*They do not act with their children as I do with ours. I was brought up by my Mum with her rules, the children were expected to help her in all daily chores and the older ones would help her care for the younger ones. Mum was very strong; she needed to be to keep the nine of us in order and the house up together. Everyone was expected to pull their weight. It may be my condition but I thought that Mum's conditioning was the correct way to behave. Throughout my life I have thought it and I don't understand why men are the way they are. It was quite a shock, and still is in fact; to find out that this was not the way a man was 'supposed' to act. When I was*

81

about 18 and at work it really hit home that men were meant to act in a certain way, all bravado and status, it makes no logical sense at all. It just wasn't a nice way to behave. It doesn't compute; I am more confused than ever I was".

He doesn't understand why fathers don't interact more with their children, taking an interest in their lives, helping them with projects and hobbies, playing games such as Xbox, Wii or rollerblading, encouraging them to broaden their horizons and giving them good moral and social rules, money sense and a good work ethic to help them in the future. Max does all of these and much more because that is what he considers his duty as a father to be, and he enjoys interacting with them and having fun. It is great to watch them together, Max does far more with them than their biological father ever did and he has certainly transformed the way they behave in the home and in particular with me. They understand the need to help around the house with day to day things and have each got chores to do. The older ones respect him and how he has put rules into the household. They know that they must abide by the house rules and wouldn't dare be disrespectful to me or flout the rules. They also value Max's opinion on a variety of subjects ranging from the practical to the personal. It is so lovely watching them have manly banter, they are friends, but they are also respectful of the fact he is their step dad. Soon after we were engaged William, the eldest, started to introduce Max as his step dad when we met him in town with his friends and this really made Max very happy. William had not been prompted he just did it; not long after this we were in town, and one of William's friends came up to talk to us and he introduced us to his friends as William's Mum and Dad, this really made Max happy and gave him a feeling of fitting in. Now we are always viewed as Mum and Dad. Max doesn't expect the older boys to call him Dad but does expect them to treat him with respect; he is also upset if he doesn't get birthday, Christmas and Father's day cards from them. (They always remember him). These things are important to him and he always makes sure that all the children buy me cards and presents at the appropriate times. This is how a family should respect their mother which was a novelty for me, since the children's father never ensured that they remembered me at these times.

Max is very house proud; when he was on his own he obviously had a routine for every aspect of his daily life, cooking, cleaning, laundry and other such things. Since we descended on him with all our baggage, boxes of toys, books and other clutter he has had to cope. This is not easy for him at all, the children are quite untidy and tend to dump clothes and school bags where they take them off, forgetting to move them or just oblivious to the fact that they are in an inappropriate place. Hair brushes on the sofa after a hurried brush before school, shoes in the middle of the floor where they were kicked off in haste to change into trainers, DVD's left in a mess and not put back into their boxes. All these things frustrate and stress Max, he has been fantastic and, with work, the children are learning that we will not pick up after them; Max's persistence is paying off in this area. I sometimes forget when I tell them to do a certain task as soon as they come in from school, often because I am focussed on cooking the tea, but Max knows that there is a routine to be maintained and he spots instantly what needs to be done, and insists it is done immediately and not "in a minute" which is the usual cry. Max's need for order and routine is helping the family live together in a very confined space and teaching the children that they must take responsibility for their own possessions.

Max has a real knack of embarrassing the children in front of their friends. One evening we were about to take Charlotte and two of her friends to the supermarket. Max has his iphone in a case which opens like a book and something one of the girls said triggered a thought about WALL.E, a film about a robot, he put the open iphone case over his eyes like a visor and said "Wall.E" several times. He looked really funny so Patrick and I laughed but Charlotte was horrified and her friends puzzled. The more she complained the worse he got. We went to the supermarket and soon after we went in he started again with the WALL.E impression. He was doing it in front of the shoppers and Charlotte was so embarrassed she had to walk off with her friends. She will normally cope with his 'childish' and 'silly' behaviour, her words, but in front of friends she finds it extremely difficult and Max knows this but won't give up, he doesn't realise the upset he is causing her and if I try to tell him he just tells me not to be silly, that's she's ok. This can be quite difficult for me, I find Max's behaviour amusing and harmless fun, he often does this with me and the location has no influence on his behaviour as it is spontaneous, happening as a result of a trigger word or action. He used to keep this spontaneity in check in public but, because I am ok with the behaviour, he feels safe to do it, which goes some way to easing his stress. But it is difficult watching the children struggling to understand why he persists in his actions, I know that it is just him having fun and relaxing, which is fine with me, but he really cannot understand that he is causing them stress and should stop.

"Children can be quite egotistical and often selfish, and if child and adult are running on the same emotional level neither will want to put the other first. If you offer a child a bag of sweets he is unlikely to take the smallest one and leave you the biggest, putting your needs first;

unfortunately neither will the AS adult". Maxine Ason (2003) 'Asperger's in Love': Couple Relationships and Family Affairs. London Jessica Kingsley Publishers.

This is exactly how Max is, he will always take the largest or nicest thing; he would not consider offering it to the children and will make a comment if they take it. The children often find this quite hard to deal with and I am constantly trying to excuse his actions. Interestingly he often says the children are selfish if they don't offer to make him a drink when they get themselves one, or eat sweets which they have bought without offering him one, but cannot see that his own behaviour could be considered in the same light. He believes that as an adult it is his prerogative and the children should accept that. It is difficult for me as I always select the smallest portion or the squashed cake, and share everything as fairly as possible so that everyone else has the best.

Chapter 12

Sayings and habits

There are many things that fall into several categories and sayings could be classed as obsessions as they are repeated frequently. When he remembers something or I say something familiar it triggers a phrase. If I do not follow the expected response then he asks me to follow the 'normal' pattern. An example is

Max "*I am not well*"

Annie "I knoooow", the significance is that the word 'know' is drawn out. If I don't say it in just the correct tone and fashion, then I must keep repeating it until I get it right. It is important to him, he says he likes it; it comforts him and makes him feel better. He likes the sound and likes to hear certain things over and over again.

A long time ago we started one of these sayings which is repeated frequently and has to be done accurately or I have to start at the beginning again. It goes like this, I start by saying, "I love you." "*You always say that.*" "That's because I do." "*You always say that too.*" It is silly but it is a routine now and it can't be changed unless I add something onto the end of it, which I have no intention of doing and am very careful about this as it could end up lasting hours!

Max 'stores' phrases, sayings from TV, films, a situation etc, and uses them in everyday conversations.

"The child often has a fascination with the meanings or sounds of words and an ambiguous phrase is intriguing, causing genuine humour as occurs with puns" Asperger's Syndrome Tony Attwood.

The word 'condensation' can be repeated over and over again, this comes from an episode of 'Family guy'. These recollections of words or phrases can happen very spontaneously anywhere, we can be walking through a shopping centre, watching a film or sitting on a beach, and something will trigger a memory of a word or phrase, which is repeated exactly with the correct accent and where appropriate actions. It is not always obvious to either of us what has triggered it without us retracing the last few minutes of events. Once he has said it, he will ask me where the word or phrase came from and I have to try and remember the correct film or programme. The accent he uses or action, if any, that accompanies the phrase can sometimes give me a clue but I still find it really hard to do unless he has used the phrase recently, as I do not have the same interest in the odd piece of information from a film rather the whole film. He often gets frustrated with me if he thinks it is one that I should remember, regardless of the fact that it has popped up randomly with no obvious connection to our current surroundings. The details that are in his head are so obvious to him, but not to me. It is a game that he enjoys and we play a lot since he is constantly reminded of things.

TV learning

This has done wonders for Max in many ways. He has picked up lots of information about the world and social interactions, although these have not always been typical of everyday life. In other ways it has crippled him especially his echolalia. As I write this he is blowing raspberries and asking me to say Meg, a 'joke' from 'Family Guy'. He says that the raspberry blowing relaxes him because it feels nice. He gets uncontrollable urges to repeat certain phrases or actions at random moments. He usually keeps it check in front of other people, as he has learnt that most people do not approve of, or understand it, although this causes him great stress which, before me, he would vent at home behind closed doors, safe inside his inner bubble. Now, because he is relaxed around me, he is happier to allow me to share in this which is a great honour and one which no one else has been afforded.

Delayed Echolalia

Delayed echolalia has been defined as the "echoing of a phrase after some delay or lapse of time. Persons with autism who repeat TV commercials, favorite movie scripts, or parental reprimands come to mind when we think of delayed echolalia. Delayed echolalia appears to tap into long-term auditory memory, and for this reason, may be a different phenomenon from immediate echolalia. Because it can involve the recitation of entire scripts, delayed echolalia, is often thought to denote evidence of near genius intellect. This may or may not be the case. Delayed echolalia may be interactive or no interactive and may be used with no intent or purpose or may have a very specific purpose for the individual. There appears to be more potential functions for delayed echolalia than were found for immediate echolalia. A key to understanding the specific use of delayed echolalia in any individual is awareness of the individual's daily behaviour and familiarity with their verbalizations. Many children with autism become experts not just at echoing the content of what is said by others but also the voice, inflexion, and manner in which the words were originally spoken. The value of echolalia for the person may be that the echoed words and significant cues become stored information for the person to refer to later as internal rehearsal of the event:

http://www.brighttots.com/Echolalia_Child_Autism

Max nearly *"f***ed"* his degree because of his phrase storing habits. He had to read a lot of books whilst studying and, as a result, 'collected' sentences not to use, but just because he liked the way they were constructed and sounded when they were used. When his tutor told him that he thought Max had plagiarised some of his essays he couldn't believe it. He hadn't done it deliberately he just liked the sentence and the way it was constructed. He didn't even use it in the same context as it had been used originally.

Max is excellent at 3D copying, *"It's easy because you are simply following the lines. You are just transposing the lines, I can just do it. There is no emotional involvement what is important is accuracy."* He is very accurate and good at profiles, but cannot draw someone face on. He had no idea he could draw like that; it was when he was messing about with chalk on a chalk board one day and decided to try and draw someone's profile that he realised his ability.

Religion is a subject that he uses constantly to tease me. He is Roman Catholic and I am Church of England, my father was a vicar. Max takes great delight in winding me up over our religious differences.
For example: *"Mine is the proper religion and I will definitely go to heaven as God loves the Catholics the best"*. Initially I would play the game, not that I could win! He always has the last word but that is fine as he really enjoys the game. It started to become less enjoyable when he said I was '*biting*', and then started to tell friends that I always bit when he talked about religion. I am not overly religious, despite my father being a vicar, but I do have a thorough knowledge of several religions, through my Father, good schooling and having taught RE at a secondary school, and have a healthy respect for all of

them. I am well versed but do not hold strong religious beliefs apart from a broad Christian belief and an interest in Buddhism. Max too leans towards the gentle Buddhist teachings, having been taught a lot by John, his friend and mentor. Now I find it easier to agree with Max and not discuss, unfortunately it ruins his game, *"You are no fun"*, but I do find it difficult as discussing and playing games is fun, but being told you are "biting" is not, as it is no longer a game or any fun.

Blowing raspberries.

Max will blow raspberries in front of me after he has had a few drinks; when we chatted about this he said, *"I didn't need to have a few drinks to blow raspberries before you, I would do them all the time at home, I liked the sensation and the noise. I also used to bang my head on my pillow, not because I was mad just because I liked the timing and repetitiveness of it. I am ashamed and embarrassed that I liked and enjoyed doing it. I couldn't see any harm in it but knew that people do not accept this kind of thing; it is not acceptable in public so I face a huge struggle every day to stop the urges. I don't feel mental but know that I am. I am truly embarrassed because, when I see people with mental problems out and about doing weird things I make comments about them, but I really think fair play and wish that I could do my things in public. I do it behind closed doors, this has become even more difficult because I am rarely alone at home anymore, and my secret life is more restricted than ever. I shouldn't judge people when I know I like doing it."*

Chapter 13

Day to day things

STIMS also known as Stereotypy

Sense	Stimming Actions
Visual	Flapping hands, blinking and / or moving fingers in front of eyes; staring repetitively at a light
Auditory	Making vocal sounds; snapping fingers
Tactile	Scratching; rubbing the skin with one's hands or with an external object
Vestibular	Moving body in rhythmic motion; rocking front and back or side-to-side
Taste	Licking body parts; licking an object
Smell	Smelling objects or hands; other people

http://autism.wikia.com/wiki/Stimming

Self-stimulatory (repetitive / physical) behaviours.

Max has several of these and at first they were difficult to get used to, but they are part of him and I just accept them now. They become a lot worse the more stressed he is. He remembers that as a child he used to move his fingers in front of his eyes studying them closely. He thought that they looked different from the rest of his body as if they didn't belong. *"I used to stare at them hoping that they would answer my questions"*. He has stopped this as he has got older but still retains many of his other STIM's.

He 'cracks' his thumb joints. He has to 'crack' both and will keep fiddling until both are done. Repetitive movements, these are most obvious in bed as it is quiet and the sound seems enhanced. He rubs his foot against his shin. *"The rubbing would last a lot longer if you weren't around, a human in the room makes me think that it's not normal but when I am on my own there is no judge. I don't get the chance to be alone anymore"*. He flicks his big toe against the next one, and rubs his shins together, lies on his stomach and raises his leg at the knee letting it fall heavily back onto the bed and many others. These may last for several minutes or much longer either, one in particular or a combination of several running one after another. Echolalia is also grouped as a STIM and is discussed separately.

Max tells me that during childhood he would rock or bang his head against the pillow as these things were very comforting for him, their repetitive nature helps him to relax. *"I absolutely loved it, it was my playtime"*. Now he feels unable to do some of these things as he considers them odd and unacceptable even *'mental'*. I have tried to say I do not mind him doing them as I know it is very comforting for him; he is gradually beginning to use a few more when I am around. When he was younger at home with his family he would bang his head against the back of the sofa or rock back and forwards on it, one of his younger sisters has told me that they thought it was a

92

game so would copy it. The subject had come up when we were generally talking about their home life with his sister and this had been mentioned, I felt a little awkward as I knew it was not a game, it was because of his Asperger's and he was obviously stressed at the time and needed to relax. I have no idea how having them copy him made him feel but it can't have been easy. He says that, "*I don't remember feeling difficult when my sisters copied me; I guess I was in my own world so was fairly oblivious of what they were doing*". We noticed this habit of rocking a few months ago in one of his younger brothers, when we attended a family wedding. We knew that he was not happy attending the wedding and this manifested itself in an obvious rocking motion, which I am sure he was totally unaware of.

I know that some people are not naturally able to relax when their partner does unusual things, this is often because they are very conscious of other people's opinions. Usually the things that your partner will allow themselves to do in public are not that 'terrible', just a little unconventional, try and ignore people around you and enjoy the moment.

My advice would be to try and understand the behaviour and allow it without judgement. It is their way of dealing with our confusing world; it relaxes them and in turn helps them maintain as normal a life as they can. The more stress and confusion Max encounters the more STIM's he exhibits, but by allowing him to continue them without question or comment the easier it is for him to relax.

Max's 'bubble'

This is his safe place. There are essentially three bubbles, the inner most one is the safest and most private one, which if it were real would have a TV, Xbox and Star Trek Voyager DVD's inside, a place where he would be alone and not having to interact with anyone and the stupidity of humans. I skirt around on the edge of this inner bubble and am the only person ever to be allowed this close. Max doesn't make friends easily and it takes him about three years before he would consider them as friends he says, "*I have to understand them and get used to their ways*". If they are still close after three years they will stick around, as Max can be brutally honest and only people who accept his approach will stay. These friends are allowed to enter the middle bubble. Everyone else skirts around in the outer bubble kept as far away as possible with minimal interaction. "*They are chaotic and don't abide by the rules. My bubble is a step out of the world, the mayhem and confusion of life. That is all I can say on it, what more is there to say*". Early on in our friendship I bounced about in the outer layer of the bubble getting closer to the middle area as our relationship developed. About six months into the friendship I entered the middle bubble; this was a very fast progression so when the situation became too overwhelming I was pushed out again. Gradually he relaxed with me and I was allowed to stay in the middle bubble; when we became a couple I started to edge towards the inner bubble, I bounced around just on the outside of the inner bubble until we got engaged when he allowed me into the inner bubble. He had made his mind up that he trusted me enough to marry me so allowed me into the inner sanctum. I am still on the outer edge of the inner bubble but when Max is totally relaxed I am allowed a little closer to the centre but not for long. This is perfectly ok as I know it is a safety net and must be treated with the utmost respect, as this makes the relationship a lot easier to maintain. I allow him to retreat into the safety zone and stay there as long as is necessary as it pays dividends.

"Before I met you I was in my 'bubble' and I experienced the world as much as I could manage and then withdrew. I sought socialisation but it was restricted to being with Robert, Sally, my sister, or Sea Cadets as long as I had my safe haven to go to and recover. You have stretched me beyond where I would go, partly because I trust you and there is a safety net, but I have lost so much. I am experiencing complications that I would never have allowed before. My mind wants to go there but it is very draining, I am ashamed that I cannot cope with it. You have allowed me excitement that I could never have done on my own, it is yin and yang, I want to do these things but it causes me great pain."

"Older children with Asperger's Syndrome create imaginary worlds, especially when they cannot understand or be understood in the real world." Asperger's Syndrome. Tony Attwood.

I love to cuddle up watching a film but Max finds this really difficult, he will occasionally do it as he knows I enjoy it a lot, but he can only manage to cuddle for a maximum of twenty minutes and then feels trapped and uncomfortable and has to move back to his seat. This initially upset me as I could have cuddled him for hours enjoying the closeness and togetherness, but now I understand that he is pressurised by it. It is nothing personal and not some sort of rejection of me, just a safety mechanism to prevent him pain.

If Max has something he is supposed to do, a task or job, I have to remind him in the morning and usually send a text just before he is due to do the task because his memory is not good or he gets very distracted from his routine, this confuses him and he forgets things he has to do in the day.

Max has always had a very strong work ethic and has nearly always worked. When he was young he gave at least half his wages to his mum to help support the rest of the family as they were not well off. He felt it was his duty as the second eldest boy to help his Mum as much as he could. Interestingly none of the others contributed, but Max felt strongly that it was the right thing to do. He also gave his little sisters pocket money, until they started to expect and demand it which Max objected to and consequently stopped.

For many years, when Max was younger, he did a variety of menial jobs, holding down two or three at a time. These were mainly cleaning jobs which he liked as he was on his own and left in peace to get on with things; of course, as an AS sufferer he did them meticulously but he didn't have any real aspirations to improve himself, as he thought that he was not able, probably largely due to his low self-esteem and constant self-doubt, a legacy of having been bullied most of his life.

Focus

Monotropism or mind blindness is where the mind can only focus on a limited range of interests but that focus is intense and obsessive. Once Max is focussed he cannot easily be distracted.

Max is a perfectionist, when he does any DIY, he must have the correct tools so the job will not start until he has located the best deals on the internet, this could take some time and money. Then he will think everything through in detail using spirit levels and laser levels. The correct brushes for painting, correct nails and screws and correct power tools and the job will not start until he has everything in its place.

Once Max's mind is focussed on a particular way of doing something he is unable to change. Once, when we were doing some DIY , I wanted to try a different way because I thought I could see a problem the way Max had thought of doing it, he was so focussed he didn't even hear my attempt to offer an alternative suggestion. I had to wait until something didn't quite work out and his focus was broken before I could offer my idea. He took a moment to evaluate it and then put his own slant on it, as he had better knowledge of the tools.

"The person with Asperger's Syndrome often has difficulty with cognitive flexibility – in other words, they have a one-track mind (Minshow et al.1992). Their thinking tends to be rigid and not to adapt to change or failure. They may have only one approach to a problem and need tuition in thinking of alternatives". Tony Attwood. Asperger's Syndrome. A guide for parents and professionals.

We work extremely well together, in DIY terms, it is a bit like the expert and his lackey. There are of course problems, as he expects me to understand exactly what he is going to do and what I am expected to do to assist. In his head he can see the process, so it is completely obvious what I am expected to do and also the final outcome. Initially I found this very hard and he snapped at me often, because he was frustrated that I hadn't handed him the correct tool at the right moment, or pointed the torch at the appropriate spot instantly, however, as I got more familiar with the way he worked and the tools we were using, I could second guess what he was expecting of me and we started to have fun. I still had to be very patient when I got something wrong or didn't understand his instruction, as he would snap at me as if I was a total imbecile or had deliberately misunderstood his instructions. The trick was not to take it personally and accept that I had messed up and carry on according to his instructions. I got extremely good at using the power tools as Max is a very good teacher, explaining and demonstrating exactly how to use them. Our best bit of teamwork was cutting skirting board. Max cannot work out the angles for the corners but I found them easy to visualise so together we flew through each room doing a very professional job. He also struggles with measuring but together we overcome these problems. Tiling is absolutely accurate he uses a laser spirit level and a professional tile cutter.

Dyslexia

"A significant proportion of children with Asperger's Syndrome tend to be at the extremes of ability in the areas of reading, spelling and numbers. Some develop hyperlexia, that is, highly developed word recognition, but very poor comprehension of the words or storyline (Tirosh and Canby 1993), while others have considerable difficulty cracking the code of reading. Hans Asperger (1944) referred to how his original group of children included those with signs of dyslexia and difficulty learning to spell. In contrast some were fascinated by numbers from an early age and were extraordinarily precocious in their ability to count."
Asperger's Syndrome. Tony Attwood.

Max was diagnosed with dyslexia very late in life whilst at university and had struggled for years throughout his school life and into working life. At school he found it hard to follow what the teachers were saying, especially if they were talking whilst he was trying to copy things from the board, a task he found almost impossible because of the dyslexia, and frustrating because often it was rubbed off long before he had completed copying it. If he was expected to listen and copy from the board or write notes, it was pointless as his focus can only be on one thing at a time, so often he froze completely, unable to do anything. Add to this the fact that he becomes fixated on words or fragments of sentences which fascinate him, and blanks out everything else until he has made sense of it, school was very difficult. He did not enjoy reading at all as he had to continuously re read passages before the information was processed and understood. He is gradually getting better and since starting to write this book, he has become fascinated with the books I have been reading and using for research. He will also read books and magazines on Egypt. his passion, or to put it more correctly obsession. This has been a lifelong interest but most of the research until recently has been confined to TV programmes and DVD's. The books have opened up a new avenue of research and he persists because he knows that the information he wants is inside, this is exactly what he did at university. Another area he finds very difficult to understand is mathematics. He has never enjoyed anything to do with mathematics as the numbers all merge into one and confuse him, he has number blindness. He is obviously able to use figures on a daily level but tries to avoid them where possible. When the children need help then he defaults to me.

Memory

Max has a very accurate memory in some areas and can give accurate and detailed descriptions of his childhood. He gets very frustrated when his sisters tell a different story, or place them in a story which they had not been involved in or were only very young when it occurred. He will correct them and take out the flowery bits. The way Max tells it is no less interesting, mainly because he remembers such incredible details, things which most people would not see or consider significant.

He remembers an incident with a child at school which happened many years ago. Max liked hot showers and the boy, Gary, cold ones. Gary tried to turn the shower down and so Max turned it back up, this carried on for a while before they started fighting and a teacher broke it up. At break time Gary had another go at Max and lost, this was the only fight Max can remember that was about him. Gary was on the outskirts of a local gang, and at lunchtime Max was challenged to a fight with a large 'fat' kid who was one of the top gang members. Max didn't want to fight because his gripe wasn't with this kid, it was with Gary. Because Max wouldn't fight the kid he got beaten up. He had no desire to do damage to the 'fat' kid so wouldn't fight. It was a wet day and Max's trousers got soaked so he had an excuse to get out of school and go home.

One day 'Piggy Palmer' the *'hardest'* kid in school was having a go at one of Max's younger brothers near their home. When Max got there he realised, *"Oh s**t that's only Piggy Palmer the hardest kid in school"* Max tackled him. *"Luckily a neighbour came out and stopped the fight. If I were honest, which I am, if the neighbour hadn't come out I would have lost the fight. From that time on I had a lot of respect from Piggy Palmer he would say,* "I have a lot of respect for you" *to me!"* Piggy Palmer came from a notorious gang on the estate and there was even a TV documentary made about him later.

Another incident Max can remember happened at school, when the *'hardest'* girl in the school tried to push into the queue for the ice-cream van. *"My Mum always told me that if a girl wants to play like a boy then she has to take the consequences"*. Max told her to go to the back of the queue. She got aggressive so Max *'decked'* her. She had broken the rule and the rules were more important to Max than the person was. He remembers one night outside a taxi office when a very drunk girl started accusing a man of staring at her, the man ignored her and so she got up and smacked him in the face three times. The man wouldn't hit her and Max couldn't understand why he wasn't defending himself and hitting her back. *"Why would anyone accept that, he didn't even bring his arms up to defend himself, it was sickening to watch and if I hadn't been so traumatised watching it I would have gone in there and stopped her, I don't get it"*.

Max has a very strong sense of what is right and wrong, much of this has come from his mother who instilled in him the correct way to behave and a strong moral code. This becomes very apparent in everyday living when he interacts with, or watches people going about their daily business. He often cannot understand why people react or not in certain situations. The previous examples indicate that this coding started early in life. He had no desire to hit a boy with whom he had no issue, the girl in the ice cream queue shouldn't have pushed in and the man should have defended himself because he had done nothing wrong.

From a personal point of view, Max struggled really hard with the concept that I was technically married when we first got together, despite the fact that I was not living with my ex-husband, had not been for eight months and was eight months into divorce proceedings, so was definitely not going back to him. He kept trying to find out online and from family and friends what was a legally acceptable time frame for us to start a relationship, and subsequently move in together, because on paper I was still a married woman. I am sure that he would have been far happier if I had been divorced before we got together, as it would have been clear cut and correct with no grey areas. He is also very particular about saying please and thank you and

101

other common courtesies, these were expected and demanded by his mother and therefore cannot be changed. I remember a similar upbringing and have always tried to instil these qualities into my own children, as courtesy costs nothing and makes a huge difference, so on this one we are in total agreement. This inherent code of conduct has both good and bad sides, as sometimes he takes it to extremes, or has set himself a slightly odd code that doesn't fully fit with society's demands. For example he believes in total honesty and finds 'white lies' very difficult and unnecessary. He can be quite brutal in his delivery and doesn't flower things up, he just says it as it is, which for some people can be quite disconcerting. Examples of this 'brutal honesty' can be found under that heading.

"Once codes of conduct are explained then the child often rigidly enforces them, perhaps becoming the class policeman, honest to a fault when such behaviour actually breaks the code of conduct. For example, in class the teacher was distracted and a child was deliberately misbehaving to the delight of the other children. The teacher realised someone had just been disobedient and asked, 'Who did that?' There was a long silence, broken by the child with Asperger's Syndrome who helpfully announced who had misbehaved, unaware of the glares of disapproval from the other children as he had broken the code of silence". Tony Attwood Asperger's Syndrome. A guide for parents and professionals.

Lying,

"Why do people do this? I can see right through it, I don't understand why they are doing it."

Max has experienced this all his life and, although he

knows it is happening, he has no idea why people can't just tell the truth.

Probably the lie that has had the most devastating effect on both of us happened very recently. Our dream has been to live in Egypt, taking the youngest children with us and any of the older ones who wish to start a new life in a beautiful and developing land. Our plans were temporarily scuppered with the recession as both our houses lost all their equity which we were using to buy in Egypt. We had been helping one of Max's sisters through a particularly difficult patch, both financially and emotionally, during her divorce. She asked us how we were getting on with our plans to move. We told her that we had put it all on hold for a while. A few days later she popped round and said she had been thinking and would like to suggest a proposition. Her divorce settlement would be quite sizeable and she would like to help us with our dream. She proposed that she would buy the house that we wanted and our flat, which she loved, and once we had established ourselves and I had found a teaching job we could start to pay her back. Max begged her not to make the offer but she persisted and over the next few weeks the dream started to gather momentum. The house we had looked at was very large and had a three bed, self-contained flat which we could rent out, we would organise the clientele and take them on trips, and she would take the money as payment for the house, thus getting the loan paid off far quicker. It all seemed perfect, she thought it would be a wonderful investment and we would have our dream. Max and I looked at it from every angle and, although we had been sceptical initially, it seemed that we would all benefit from the plan. Several months went past and more plans were made. Max and I were becoming more excited and hopeful that we would be in Egypt sooner than we had thought; the initial doubts were gradually being dispelled by her enthusiasm. One afternoon I was picking Patrick up from school and noticed that Max's sister's house had a sold sign up outside. We were puzzled but assumed that the money was taking time to process because of the difficult nature of the divorce. After a couple of weeks with no contact from his sister, despite sending a couple of text's, we decided to pop over to see his other sister; she told us that the house had been sold and the money was being spent on setting up a business for their sister's partner. We were devastated. Max on the one hand couldn't believe that his own sister had totally lied to him and deceived him over such an important thing, and on the other hand, he said he had known that she would not do it and knew that it was all a lie, *"because that's what humans do"*. He had begged her several times not to make the promise if she wasn't one hundred percent certain that she would go through with it. Max has been devastated, his depression got worse; he spent hours on 'You Tube' watching videos of Egypt and on sites selling houses to see if he could find one that we could afford. Not an option since we have no equity in the flat and no savings, yet still he searches, he is unable to move on and his anger at his sister is immense. He will never talk to her again as he feels what she has done is unforgivable. He says that it bears out his belief that all humans lie and that is why he does not trust anyone. *"If your own sister can do this to you then anyone will"*.

Max has been lied to all his life, which is something that is understood, although not usually considered acceptable by most people, but for Max it is more than just unacceptable, *"It is a rule, a law,"* he finds it difficult to rationalise, *"Why would anyone want to deceive another person, if you don't want to do something then say so, after all we are always told that lying is wrong so how can it be right"*. His mother instilled this in him from a very young age.

104

Until he met me and started to realise that I did not lie to him, he had believed that all humans naturally lied. His renewed belief in the possibility that some humans were different, allowed him to start to trust his sister as she was very convincing. Plus she was talking about our dream of a new life, one which Max has desperately wanted for a long time; it is his passion and obsession, this possibly encouraged him to want to believe her. Had she just made the offer and not kept revisiting it, enlarging on the plans, perpetuating our belief that she was as keen in the idea as we were, then Max would have just taken it as her trying to be nice, but, by the mere fact that she added to it with feasible ideas, she appeared sincere. What her motives were for doing such a cruel thing have totally bewildered us, but Max now firmly believes that she had no intention of going through with the plan, bearing out his belief that all humans lie for their own benefit; he thinks she was on a power trip enjoying the hold she had over us, without any concern for what it would do to us. This is reinforced since she has never made any effort to explain why she did not follow through with her offer or offered us an apology. He cannot make any sense of this behaviour, he is the most honest person I know and if he promises to do something it is done.

How this will affect our future relationship has yet to be seen; but a lesson to be learnt from this is to be as honest and open with your AS partner as you can. It is a very fragile line that we tread and once trust is broken it is a very hard thing to regain, if ever at all.

"For people with AS trust can often either be something won very easily, or which takes a lot of time and effort to gain. The former example is often found in individuals who have yet to learn that people are not always trustworthy - that sometimes (often) people do not say

exactly what they mean, and that someone's word is not their bond. Such individuals need to be treated very carefully in order for their trust in an individual not to be disappointed. The latter example tends to be found in individuals who have almost given up on NT 'dishonesty' – it can be very difficult to know who to trust when so many times in the past the individual has been let down, lied to or treated in an unexpected way".

Patterns

Max can see patterns in information and can locate data on forms very quickly by flicking through it at great speed stopping once he spots it. He does it with photos stored on the computer and this is also true of the internet, he will scroll through lists of sites at great speed and stop instantly on the chosen site. I can read fast but it all becomes a complete blur when I watch him do it and it is also very frustrating for me as I think I am missing some vital site which could offer the information I need, however, he seems to find it far quicker using his method than I do by looking at each individual site and reading the initial information. He also gets extremely frustrated watching me trying to locate web pages in my slow and pedantic way. Considering Max is so dyslexic it is astonishing that he can pick out words and data that flies past his eyes at such great speed. He is a visual thinker with an excellent eye for detail.

"People with Asperger's Syndrome appear to have a predominantly visual style of thinking...Adults with Asperger's Syndrome have explained how they have learnt history or science by visualising events – for example, running a mental video recording of changing molecular structures. Such children can also have an extraordinary eye for detail which makes their art work quite

106

remarkable". Tony Attwood. Asperger's Syndrome. A guide for parents and professionals.

When we are watching films etc, Max will notice inconsistencies in the editing. The actor may have a different tie on when he turns around, there is a reflection in a mirror of a cameraman or a car is spotted in a film set before the invention of cars. The sort of things that are put together in programmes about film blunders. However, Max does not see this in all aspects of films. If a film is deliberately there to make the impossible possible because it is a fantasy, he will accept oddities, what he cannot accept is inaccuracies in a film. I have often found inconsistencies or things that I don't think work in a film, and he will come back with an explanation for it because, in his eyes, it is not inconsistent as the film is based on fantasy and therefore these things are allowed. In this sense he would be very good at being a continuity editor. He does not sit there looking for the inconsistencies; there is no effort involved it just happens. Often he will spot something and ask if I saw it, if I haven't he will rewind the programme so that I can see the error.

Max is very gifted at art and spends hours doodling during meetings when he gets bored, it also helps his focus. These doodles are very free and organic in nature they are usually in one colour as this is the only pen he has but on occasion he will use two colours. The pieces are flowing and very beautiful, he has a desire to transfer them onto canvas but is worried that they will not turn out correctly, he is a perfectionist and although they are doodles, the lines are precise and crisp.

Tony Attwood, *"has met several famous professors and a Nobel Prize winner who have Asperger's Syndrome. Thus the thinking is different, potentially highly original, often misunderstood, but is not defective...Great advances in science and art have been attributable to people with Asperger's Syndrome."* Asperger's Syndrome Tony Attwood.

Rhythm

Is something described by Attwood as problematic.

"When Hans Asperger (1991) originally defined the features of the syndrome, he described a child who had significant problems copying various rhythms...This explains a feature that is quite conspicuous when walking next to a person with Asperger's Syndrome. As two people walk side by side they tend to synchronise the movements of their limbs, much as occurs when soldiers are on parade. Their movements have the same rhythm. The person with Asperger's appears to walk to the beat of a different drum. This can also affect the person's ability to play an instrument". Tony Attwood. Asperger's Syndrome. A Guide for Parents and Professionals. 1998.

Max has an excellent sense of rhythm and timing, having played bugle in the cadet marching band and taught drill and piping to competition level.

As a child he used to lie in bed at night and listen to music in his head. He describes it as his playtime. It was classical and yet his mother and the family did not have this type of music in the house. It wasn't until he was an adult and was with John, that he heard his first violin concerto. He cried because he realised that this was what he had been creating as a child, he had forgotten about it until he heard the same sounds that he had heard as a child. He describes composing the music in his head from scratch, absolutely amazing, and taking total focus. He would start with one instrument and add others as it progressed ending up with a full orchestra, "*It was so easy to do it, it just flowed from start to finish and I loved it*". Before he heard the violin concerto he had had a passion for the violins in his compositions. I have a love of classical music so we both enjoy evenings with the classics.

He has also found great solace walking in the countryside, this sounds perfectly normal until you find out that this is done in his head, he shuts everything else out and goes for a walk.

His creativity extends to inventing fabulous stories for cadets at camp, ensuring that he included their names and characters in the yarn, and lengthy puppet shows for our daughter with all the accents for each character, she adores them and would have one every night if she could, but this is far too draining for him.

Another example of his imagination is his constant requests for me to "*imagine if....what would you do*". This 'game' entails him asking me to imagine a scenario where something has happened to him, and I have to decide how I would react. Examples include "*Imagine if I had no legs what would you do?*" or "*imagine if I had millions in the bank and hadn't told you, what you would do?*" These questions illicit lengthy discussions, usually involving me giving a simple answer and him throwing in another problem, or challenging what I have just suggested. It is a game which he thoroughly enjoys making the scenario's more and more bizarre and complicated with each answer I give. He has a new twist for everything I have to say, it is great fun and challenges my brain.

Useless information

This is another skill of Max's; I call it useless because he cannot recall it when needed, so would be no good in a quiz setting. It seems to suddenly jump into his mind at almost random moments, if I really think about it I can usually find the trigger for the recollection but it is often not a direct route. A simple example is that the song by Elvis "I did it my way," is the most sung song. I was doing a crossword and when I finished it I said, "I did it", He broke into song singing 'I did it my way' then said *"did you know that is the most sung song"*. If he had been asked what the most sung song was in a quiz, he would not have been able to recall this information because he had been put on the spot.

Depression

When Max had his first recognised bout of depression, Star Trek Voyager got him through it. He shut himself away from the world and disappeared into the fantasy world of deep space and new galaxies. *"At the time I was dealing with people, who were autistic people, I was working in a home for Autistic people and I found them totally illogical. It was strange that I got into a job with the Autistic society because at that point I hadn't been diagnosed, quite ironic really. I couldn't make any sense of it at all; I think it was because of the sudden emotional outbursts, they made no sense at all"*. With hindsight and his diagnosis Max now questions whether it is right to put all these people with Autism together in the same room, as they would have even more problems coping with each other's outbursts and erratic behaviour than he does. *"It is almost cruel but at the end of the day it no doubt comes down to financial issues"*.

Max has suffered from diagnosed depression for many years and I think, almost certainly, for a lot longer than the diagnosis suggests. Life has been a constant uphill battle for him, and the more I learn about the condition the more I realise the difficulties it throws at him daily. He has no knowledge of any of his family having been diagnosed, but admits that he never really concerned himself with what other people were doing.

The current bout started when his workload suddenly increased massively. Up until this point he had been coping, having good routines in place. Suddenly, because of his excellent reputation for getting the job done, it was decided that he should take on the two most challenging schools in the county. This involved large quantities of paperwork and many more meetings, requiring reports to be written and parents to be interviewed. At this point no one knew about his dyslexia and the problems that it posed much less the Asperger's. He managed to keep going for a while then gradually I saw the tell-tale signs of stress developing. His started sleeping more and more and withdrew from company whenever possible. He was less affectionate and more easily annoyed. Eventually he took time off work sick and I made him go to the doctors where he was diagnosed with depression and given a month off. On returning to the doctor another month off sick was prescribed along with tablets. Eventually occupational health became involved and he had a further month off with a recommendation that he had a staged return to work, once they had arranged for him to have assistance in the form of a personal assistant and a specialised computer to help with his dyslexia. What they were missing, because of Max's refusal to mention it, was his Asperger's. The workload would have been a mammoth enough task for someone without Asperger's and dyslexia. It is hard enough for him to make sense of day to day life and all its social complexities and pitfalls, without having work piled onto him without any regard for his needs. He has to review every day, to make any sense of it, going over and over the conversations and encounters he has had trying to translate them into 'Max speak'. As the workload increased and the depression increased, things became harder and harder to translate, until eventually he couldn't cope anymore and he virtually shut down. Had we not have been living with him, I do not think it would have come to a head so quickly, as he would have just hidden in his bubble every evening and all weekend and recharged a little, without the demands of the family to stop him.

Max has the ability to be totally objective, there is no emotional floweriness just pure logic. I have often likened him to Data or Tuvak from Star Trek, an android and a Vulcan. Interestingly I have subsequently read in Asperger Syndrome by Tony Attwood, that many AS men like the logical role of Data.

"The intense interest in a person can be used as an opportunity to learn about feelings, friendships and codes of behaviour. One character quite popular with adults with Asperger's Syndrome is 'Data', who features in the recent Star Trek series. He is an android that has remarkable intellectual abilities but longs to be human. He has particular difficulty understanding human courtship, emotions and humour. The difficulties he faces are very similar to those of many adults with Asperger's Syndrome so no wonder he becomes their hero as they can empathise with his problems."Asperger's Syndrome A guide for parents and professionals. Tony Attwood 1998

One evening Max asked me who I thought I would liken myself to, from Star Trek and I said B'Elana or Seven of Nine. I like the feistiness of B'Elana and the efficiency of

Seven. When asked, Max chose Data, Tuvak and Tom Paris. These three fit him perfectly and interestingly B'Elana and Tom are a couple so now, when we watch the episodes, he talks as if we are Paris and B'Elana

Max says he chose these characters because, "*I found that I could relate to Data and Tuvak because when they talk, and the way they talk, is exactly the same way that I think, it could be me talking*". Tom Paris is daring, exciting and loves B'Elana which is why I think he chose him.

His memory of films or TV programmes is astonishing. He can recall a whole episode of Star Trek just from watching a few seconds of the beginning sequence, or part way through he will tell me the next line exactly. An example is when B'Elana is talking to Neelix about food, Max said, "*She will ask for banana pancakes*", sure enough seconds later B'Elana asks for banana pancakes. He probably hadn't seen the episode for two or more years. This is really bizarre since he often cannot remember what happened a couple of hours before. Obviously 'banana pancakes' interested him and he remembered the context accurately. His love of Star Trek Voyager and Next Generation obviously helps this recall and often when we start to watch an episode he will ask if I want to know what happens. If I say yes I will get a complete and accurate account of the episode.

Motor skills

"Clumsiness is not unique to Asperger's Syndrome, and it occurs in association with a range of disorders of development. However, research suggests that between 50 per cent and 90 per cent of children and adults with Asperger's Syndrome have problems with motor coordination (Ehlers and Gilberg 1993; Ghaziuddin et al.

1994; Gilberg 1989; Szatmari et al. 1990; Tantum 1991)".

Max is very heavy footed. He firmly places his feet on every step when going up or down stairs which is very noisy. He knows he does this and says it is because he is fearful of tripping. This habit can cause problems particularly when returning to a small guesthouse late, when most of the other guests are elderly and have gone to sleep. Max tends to thud up the stairs and I have to remind him that people are sleeping. His attitude is that we are paying guests and therefore entitled to behave as we would in our own home. It is far easier and less worrying for me if we stay in large hotels with lifts and no stairs.

Handwriting is also associated with motor skills and this is an area that Max has problems with. It tends to be spidery although it is legible.

Before Max and I got together he used to have all sorts of different coloured shirts for work. He could not cope with the daily problem of deciding which colour to wear each day. In the end we got rid of them all and bought identical white ones, you would have thought this was the perfect solution and for a while it was, however as the shirts began to age he started to have the problem of which one looked newer. The solution was to throw them all away as soon as they start to look tired and buy a new set. We have one blue shirt which is worn on a Friday and signifies the end of the working week, a time that Max really looks forward to, as he knows he can start to relax and unwind over the weekend ready for the next week's onslaught. This may sound trivial to some, but it makes such a big difference to Max because choice is so difficult for him, he would rather not have it and it is such a simple thing for me to do. He lives for the holiday periods, as he works term time only, because during this extended period of rest he knows that he will start to regain some of his former self. This may sound odd but by the end of a long term he is totally mentally exhausted from trying to make sense of the world around him.

Sensory overload.

When any or all of his senses become overloaded he will just withdraw completely.

"About 40 per cent of children with autism have some abnormality of sensory sensitivity (Rimland 1990). There is now evidence to suggest that the incidence may be the same for Asperger's Syndrome (Garnett and Attwood 1995; Rimland 1990). One or several sensory systems are affected such that ordinary sensations are perceived as unbearably intense. The mere anticipation of the experience can lead to intense anxiety or panic. Fortunately the hypersensitivity often diminishes during later childhood, but for some individuals it may continue throughout their lives". Tony Attwood Asperger's Syndrome. A guide for parents and professionals.

Unfortunately Max still has problems with sensory sensitivity as they have followed him through into adult life. The main areas are smells, touch, taste, sounds and light intensity.

Smells.

"Some people with Asperger's syndrome report that specific smells can be overpowering". (Cesaroni and Garber 1991) Asperger's Syndrome. A guide for Parents and Professionals. Tony Attwood

Max has a heightened sense of smell and will often comment on something long before anyone else is aware of it. If he smells something he dislikes he reacts violently in a very childlike manner, often pull disapproving faces and making loud comments about it and looking all around him to see where it is coming from. This is fine in the house but a little embarrassing if we are in a crowded area such as a restaurant or shopping centre. Extreme reactions to a smell he dislikes have included retching over the smell of raw meat and coughing violently, or retching when smelling our son's Lynx aftershave, it makes his breathing difficult. Nice smells include fried onions and cut grass, the latter makes him feel homely.

I am very conscious of this and was told very early on in our relationship when I decided to wear some perfume that he didn't like the musky smell he prefers floral scents. We went out shopping just before Valentine's Day and I spotted a perfume shop, so suggested it would be a nice gift. We started looking around and, because I was aware of his aversion to certain smells I suggested I try some on and he could see if he liked the smell. He asked what was the point of him smelling it if I liked it. I tried to explain that he would be the one smelling it all the time, as I would get used to the scent on my body, but if he didn't like the smell it could cause a problem. He didn't accept this idea and said he wanted to go home. I started to say that I would forget about the perfume and we could look for another gift but he turned around, left the shop and headed for the car. I knew it was pointless trying to reason with him so I followed him to the car and we went home. The issue was discussed later and resolved. I received a lovely bottle of floral perfume for my birthday. It was a complete surprise, and he had chosen it with our daughter and often remarks on how nice I smell. The wonderful gift nearly caused another misunderstanding! When I opened it and sprayed it on, I was surprised at its very floral scent as I had not worn floral perfumes for many years, and stupidly said that I would have to " get used to it" having normally opted for a more musky type of scent. I have "got used to it" and love it. Expensive tastes! The comment however is mentioned frequently usually after I have put the perfume on he says, "You smell nice", and then reminds me that I didn't like it at first. I explain, again, that it wasn't a case of not liking it, just that it was unexpected. He will then say that I didn't like it and so it goes on.

Another rather disconcerting smell related occurrence happened very soon after we had got together. I had eaten something garlicky and, despite the fact I had brushed my teeth before getting into bed, he pulled a face as I leant forward to kiss him and he told me my breath smelt. Needless to say I was mortified, I could not understand how it did as I had cleaned my teeth thoroughly but it still hurt when he told me. I got up and brushed my teeth and used mouth wash but it certainly gave my confidence a knock. I try not to eat garlic etc if he is not having it as well, and brush my teeth very thoroughly. Thankfully there has not been a repeat performance.

Taste

This is a difficult one because everyone has likes and dislikes. Most people will tolerate a slightly less perfectly prepared meal; they may not enjoy it particularly, but will be polite and at least eat some of it. Max on the other hand will either like it or hate it, there is nothing in between. He has very acute taste buds and can identify individual spices, herbs and ingredients no matter how subtle in a dish with ease, and will comment on whether they work well together or not, or whether there is too much or not enough. He will notice if something is slightly burnt, if its texture is wrong, or it is different from the last time he ate it. Just as with smells the reactions will be over exaggerated. We were on holiday one year and had gone out with two other couples to a lovely restaurant for a farewell meal. I had selected a steak stuffed with blue cheese and he had a curry. Max tried it and hated it making it really obvious. I suggested we swap as I was quite happy to eat his food and he likes steak. It was a very bad move. He took one mouthful and rather than spit it subtly into a napkin he spat it out onto the plate complaining loudly and pulling faces. The blue cheese was far too strong for his taste and there was a lot of it, he loudly declared that it was disgusting, tasted as if it had gone off and he couldn't possibly eat it. I suggested we order something else for him but he was adamant he didn't want anything else; he would rather sit and eat nothing than try to finish something that was substandard. Luckily the waiter didn't come and ask us how the meal was, because Max will always tell them if he feels there are any problems. This is not to be difficult it is just accurate. In some ways I have similar views to Max, although not expressed as vehemently as he does. If I go to a restaurant and am served an expensive steak that is over cooked, I like mine very rare, then I will ask for a new one as I am not prepared to pay for something I didn't order.

I decided one evening to cook mushrooms and prawns in a creamy garlic sauce, a recipe I acquired from a wonderful restaurant after we had eaten it there several times. Max really enjoys it and I have had much success with it. On this particular evening I was distracted for a few minutes and the garlic burnt. I removed it from the pan gave it a cursory wipe and started again. Max had smelt the burning and questioned it so I explained and carried on. I finished cooking the meal and Max came into the kitchen, he smelt the pan and commented that it still smelt burnt, and asked if I had cleaned everything before starting again, I assured him that I had but he was still unsure whether he should have any. I was upset and asked if he would like something else, he declined so I sat down to eat mine. It had a very slight burnt taste but I told him it wasn't too bad. He still declined. I felt really upset that I had ruined the food and that he was not eating anything. A few days later the evening was discussed and it turned out that he had expected me to give him some, when I had come in with only a plate for me, he had thought that I was cross because he had made comments about the burnt smell and was being deliberately difficult. This obviously upset me as I felt guilty for not serving him a portion and allowing him to taste it and make his own decision.

Max will eat most foods but if there is any vinegar in it he will choke, he feels as if his windpipe is closing and he struggles for breath, coughing violently. Sometimes it is hidden in sauces and dressings so it can come as a bit of a surprise with the first mouthful, as it did the first time I saw him choking! I was really worried and he couldn't explain that he would be ok after a few minutes as he was coughing so much. Now I am more prepared and we just let it run its course. Textures will affect how Max views food, in particular he dislikes biscuits because he doesn't like crunching them he says, *"It's nasty, like someone scratching on a blackboard"*. He doesn't even like watching people eat biscuits. Shaped pasta is another food that he will not eat. He loves spaghetti and macaroni but pasta shells and twists are out of the question he thinks they taste like, *"slime"*.

Max will not eat meat that he has cooked himself; he doesn't think that it is cooked properly, even if it is burnt to a crisp he will throw it away. In the past he has bought a joint and left it in the oven for several hours tried a tiny bit and then thrown the rest away, he couldn't bear to eat it because he felt it was raw. This problem applies to all joints and chops; he has no problem with burgers, sausages, mince meat, well cooked bacon and steaks. The thinking behind the steaks was that people eat them almost raw so it should be ok. I think a lot of this stems back to his childhood when every year they would have a chicken for Christmas, and without fail he would be sick, he was the only one out of nine children who was sick. After years of experimenting, leaving out various other treats before the meal such as sweets and chocolate he eventually decided that it was the chicken and stopped eating it! Many years later he walked past a Miss Millies and liked the smell so decided to try some, he wasn't sick and started to eat chicken again but not cook it himself. When I first started to date him, I started to cook a Sunday roast and he really enjoyed it as long as I didn't ask him to have anything to do with the meat. He wouldn't even put it in the oven! Occasionally he will look closely at a piece of meat I have cooked and ask if it is cooked properly, but accepts that I know what I am doing and haven't poisoned anyone yet!

NEVER take food from his plate uninvited, nicking a chip is a big no no. It is rather like a scene from 'Gavin and Stacy' when the extended family are ordering an Indian takeaway, they ask Smithy what he would like and he makes it quite clear to them that, what he orders is for him and not for anyone else, if they want what he has ordered then they should order it themselves. This did not go down too well but is completely logical. Max believes that whatever is on your plate is yours and no one has a right to it. Occasionally if he has something unusual on his plate in a restaurant he will offer me a little to try, but I would not dream of taking it without asking. Once a friend decided to take a chip off his plate whilst they were having lunch, she was severely reprimanded in his usual blunt and to the point manner. Max was absolutely flabbergasted that someone would take something off his plate without permission. In his words, "*It was like she was stealing. Imagine you were sitting in a café eating chips and a complete stranger walked over and helped themselves to chips from your plate how would you feel? In my mind that is what it equates to it made no difference that I knew her she shouldn't have done it!*" She recounted this story to me thinking that I would agree with her and say that his actions were completely over the top, to her amazement I said that I agreed with him and people should ask before assuming they can help themselves. It is interesting that when you see this kind of behaviour on TV everyone just accepts it as the norm, maybe we are all prone to conditioning from what we watch.

Touch

It is better for me to limit the amount I touch him, he would rather not be touched at all than touched all but can cope with a little physical contact.

I have often watched old couples walking along holding hands, and thought how utterly wonderful and romantic it was to get to your twilight years and still hold hands. I never imagined that I could ever be in such a fortunate position, however I am now but, as I am sure you have realised, it is not that simple. For Max it is a perfectly normal thing for a couple to hold hands whilst out walking and it has also formed part of our routine and therefore one which will continue forever. It is a fun thought to think that in years to come a young person may look at us and think how romantic we look. I do however; have to hold Max's hand in a particular way, if I do not get it right he will reposition my thumb or fingers until they are in the right place. This also applies to walking arm in arm. It is not Max being picky it actually causes him pain. One weekend we walked for miles arm in arm and for the next few weeks I could not touch his arm in that place, as he felt physical pain; it was really sensitive and irritated him immensely. Despite this I know I am extremely lucky, as many people with Asperger's Syndrome will not allow displays of affection in public, and sometimes not even in private as you will note from the following quote.

"If you are the kind of woman who likes to hold hands on the street, or kiss on the beach at sunset, dating an Aspie is not for you. They are (generally) notoriously opposed to any public displays of affection, even public touching of any sort. Although you may think this is not a big deal, it becomes a big deal when your man refuses to hold you when you feel affectionate. It feels like deprivation and rejection, and both those things can resonate with early childhood scars and/or create new ones.
This may also happen in private. Some men say they don't like the feel of holding hands. Physical sensation is highly sensitized for an AS person. Some are so sensitive that even eye contact can 'hurt' while others just don't see the point of kissing and hugging." 22 things a woman must know if she loves a man with Asperger's Syndrome. Rudy Simone 2009.

Max does not have a problem with this, for which I am very grateful, as it is a chance for us to feel close and together as a couple.

However, if I had met him when he was in his twenties and even until very recently then the situation would have been very different, as then he would not entertain any thoughts of displays of public affection. He cannot explain this change in attitude, except to say that he wants to please me and will endure the pain as long as he can if I am happy.

He also loves me to rub his tummy in firm, rhythmical movements finding it very soothing and comforting. I also massage his back, neck and hands to relieve tension and so relax him. I think if he had his way and my hand muscles were stronger he would enjoy me continuing for hours to sooth away his stress

"There can be an extreme sensitivity to a particular intensity of touch or touching particular parts of the body. Temple Grandin (1984) describes her acute tactile sensitivity when she was a child. 'As a baby I resisted being touched and when I became a little older I can remember stiffening, flinching, and pulling away from relatives when they hugged me,' (p.155) ' As a child I wanted to feel the comfort of being held, but then I would shrink away for fear of losing control and being engulfed when people hugged me'. (p.151) For Temple, the forms of touch used in social greetings or gestures of affection were perceived as too intense or overwhelming. Here the avoidance of social contact was due to a physiological reaction to touch, not necessarily an avoidance of being close to or sociable with others. Asperger's Syndrome. Tony Attwood

Max hates anyone touching his ears or feet, although occasionally certain parts are more sensitive than at other times, and on a rare occasion he will let me massage his feet, with his socks on of course, but if the doctor wanted to examine his feet he would refuse. I like running my fingers through his hair if I have been allowed to sit on the arm of his chair with my legs across his lap, but if I touch his ear in the process he pulls away and rubs his ear hard as if to get rid of the touch.

He also has a hard time dealing with social touching, such as women trying to kiss him on the cheek when they meet him or men shaking his hand, he would prefer that they didn't do it as it is uncomfortable for him. He wouldn't normally offer a handshake or volunteer to kiss a woman's cheek but would do it if he felt it would help me in a social situation.

Max cannot cope with crowds. Rather than ease his way through, he will wait for a gap to appear that is large enough for him to walk through without touching anyone else. He will stand there for ages, this became very obvious when we started going to nightclubs; he went to the bar for drinks and took ages to come back, I went looking for him and found him standing the other side of a large group of people who were chatting, and had no intention of moving out of the way without someone asking them. I touched the back of one of them and said excuse me and they moved. I rescued Max and he followed me back through the gap. Now I will go ahead of him and clear the way, he keeps close so that the gap doesn't close behind me and he loses me. It usually works but I do keep checking that he is still there.

Sounds

Max is fascinated by sound, it is like playtime to him, it isn't necessarily music it could be a rhythm, a whine, scratching sound in fact anything could attract his attention, and then he will copy it and play with the sounds building them into a tune. He can hear two or three notes or words of a song and instantly remember the melody, not the singer or where he heard it just the melody or lyrics. Occasionally he will associate the melody to a time or place where he first heard it. He will hear songs on the radio or in clubs and want them for his iphone. So the search starts, this is usually very difficult as he will normally only have focussed on a few of the lyrics, rather than listening to the rest of the song for clues about the title. The artist for one such song which he had searched for for a long time, was provided by one of Charlotte's friends when he was taking her home one day. He heard the song on the radio and asked the girl if she knew what it was, which she did. He phoned me immediately and said, *"Remember 'Dynamite'"* and hung up. On his return all was revealed and he downloaded it immediately. Happy days.

Max is very sensitive to sudden loud noises in the incorrect setting. I say this because he can tolerate loud music and chatter in nightclubs without any problem, as this is where it is supposed to happen and is expected. Lots of children all chatting, shouting or screaming in high pitched voices in the house or other social setting is completely disrupting and unsettling, so he usually takes himself off to the sanctuary of his bed, away from it all. If he hears sudden high pitched noises he will cover his ears and look distressed.

There are three categories which distress him: Sudden, unexpected sounds like a dog barking or a balloon popping, high pitched continuous noises like an electric motor or confusing, complex noises found in shopping centres or social places, as he has difficulty screening out background noise and focussing on an individual. These confusing or complicated noises are not usually ones which annoy people, as they are generally experienced in areas where there are a lot of people and so an expected level of noise. Tony Attwood offers us an analogy to help us better understand how distressing these noises can be to the Asperger sufferer…

"…a suitable analogy for what it may feel like is the natural discomfort many of us have to specific sounds such as the noise of fingernails scraping down a school blackboard. The mere thought of this sound can make some people shiver." Asperger's Syndrome Tony Attwood

He has a heightened sensitivity to very faint sounds and can hear them long before anyone else.

"One young child with Asperger's Syndrome was about to leave the clinic when he suddenly and inexplicably became upset, and was unable to explain why. However the author knew of his auditory sensitivity and walked down the corridor in search of the source of the child's distress. In the ladies' toilet someone had switched on the hot air hand dryer, a sound that from the clinic was imperceptible to others, but clearly audible and perceived as too intense to the child". Asperger's Syndrome Tony Attwood.

Max is very sensitive to bright light and will wear sunglasses even on a fairly dull day, he is also very intolerant of poor lighting, he turns the light on as soon as he gets home to ensure that the room is bright and cheerful.

Max gets great enjoyment out of very simple things. His latest fascination is a small ball about 1.5 centimetres in diameter which flashes red and blue when flicked. I think it came out of a child's toy. He carries it in his shirt pocket when he goes to work and flicks it so that it shines through his pocket. He enjoys it immensely and this is a really endearing quality. It is lovely to think that in this day and age when adults are searching for more dynamic, dangerous and technological thrill seeking challenges to excite them, he can find something so simple to engage him. It is a bit like giving a toddler the box that a toy came in and watching them get hours of fun out of it.

Sleeping

Some AS suffer from insomnia, Max on the other hand could sleep for England and often takes a nap for a couple of hours when he comes in from work, or in the daytime when he is not working, 3-4 hours at the weekend. This is his way of recovering from the day and recharging in preparation for all the new challenges and uncertainties. It prevents a total overload of sensory information. He finds that as he lies in bed he can start to unravel the complexities and inconsistencies of the day, and try to make some sense of it all. When he doesn't have to get up for work or an appointment he will often lie in until 1500, or later if we have had a late night. I find this frustrating at times as, when the children are not around, I want to spend my time with him but I know that he needs to recharge his batteries. I find it impossible to lie in that long as I get a blinding headache, but I feel very frustrated that we have lost a whole precious day together. I have gone out leaving a note for him and usually return to find him still asleep and oblivious to my outing.

The more stressed Max is the more sleep he needs, his STIMS increases and his psoriasis gets considerably worse.

'Unsociable behaviour'

Max farts and burps whenever he needs to without considering where he is or who he is with. He cannot understand that most people, particularly women, do not find it socially acceptable in company. His reasoning is that he can't help it and it's a natural bodily function. Interestingly if the children do it he tells them not to!

Stubborn

Max is very stubborn and set in his ways and will rarely admit that he is wrong. When we discussed this issue he said, *"That's because I am not"*. An incredibly detailed and precise argument has to be presented if he is to change his mind. This often prevents me from entering into the sort of conversation which requires dialogue and discussion of different points of view. It is quite difficult sometimes especially when one is tired, to know that ultimately you will have to back down as you cannot 'win'.

Order

Max's sister used to call him 'Mr Trevis', this was after an old man who featured on the TV several years ago in a programme called 'Grime fighters', which was about the teams who cleaned out empty houses ready for a new tenant. Mr Trevis's house was full with the detritus of daily living and things which he would never throw away. Every room was full of stuff that he had saved over many years.

When I first started seeing Max he had a small bathroom which he was using while he constructed a new luxury bathroom. Once this was finished we took out the old bathroom and then moved all the 'stuff' which he had stored in his bedroom into the old bathroom. This consisted of a vast and varied collection of things which he had accumulated over many years, not kept for sentimental reasons, just because he had never sorted it out and had nowhere else to put it. Yet for someone who

128

doesn't like mess and prefers order it was still an interesting inconsistency in his personality. There was paperwork, saved electrical equipment, tools and much more.

We decided to move in together and this meant that we needed this room for the children so set about clearing it, putting the flooring down and generally preparing it for the children. Max had no emotional attachment to the stuff in fact if he was ever burgled, God forbid, he would not worry about what had been taken, rather the fact that someone had entered his house without permission and taken property that didn't belong to them. That is morally wrong and therefore a major issue for him. Obviously the power tools he wanted to keep for practical reasons, and also because he would have searched long and hard for the best quality that he could get, but the rest he would ruthlessly have discarded had I not insisted on sorting it as we went. I have a natural hoarding instinct so enjoyed the task, it gave me a little insight into who Max was and ensured that I saved a lot of the important paperwork, which Max would have discarded without a thought. I soon realised that Max's way of dealing with the mess was to shut the door on it so he couldn't see it.

The room progressed well and was soon ready for the children. Although Max had had his messy room, everywhere else in the house had been immaculate as a result of his meticulous cleaning routine which was shattered when we arrived.

The flat is a small Victorian ground floor property which is technically one bedroom, which we have converted into two bedrooms by using the old bathroom/box room as a second bedroom. It also has a lovely walled garden, this was totally overgrown when we moved in but now has a lawn, patio, chicken run and enough room for a ten foot inflatable pool and trampoline.

Not only did I bring with me two children, but also a huge number of boxes, these contained all I could save from my years of hoarding mementoes and treasures as the children were growing up, from the four bed house that we had lived in previously. The wide hallway suddenly became a storage area, piled in places to the ceiling and our bedroom, although initially large, was reduced to a storage room allowing very little room to manoeuvre around the bed.

The children by nature are very creative, I am a teacher of Art and Design and did a degree in textile design so it's inherited, consequently they always have an art project on the go and the living room is often covered in paints, paper and other interesting and creative equipment. They do have boxes to store everything in but when they are in the middle of things, the tendency is to leave everything out ready to carry on when they return to it.

Over the months Max and I have battled to keep things tidy making use of weekends when they are away to regroup, but the weekly chaos causes Max extreme distress, increasing his stress levels and causing him actual physical pain. This is difficult to understand for the non-AS person but he says it is painful trying to cope with, and make sense of, this constant turmoil. I am very aware of this problem, and consequently spend a lot of time nagging the children to clear up after themselves and keep our family areas tidy. They are getting better but I worry about how much more of this pressure Max can take.

As the children get older they are bringing friends home from school un announced, so Max arrives home from work to be confronted with extra children, all bubbly and noisy, in particular the girls as they have much higher pitched voices and tend to squeal when they get excited, which hurts Max's ears. He often retires to the bedroom, his sanctuary and either sleeps or goes on the computer until it is safe to come out. I do not mind this as I know this is the only way he can deal with the sudden unplanned invasion; I do miss his company, yet feel I must stay with the children to ensure they do not make too much mess or disturb Max. I do not feel it fair to ban the children from bringing friends home, although I do encourage them to ask in advance. I am quite a spontaneous person and understand why they do it, and always allowed the older ones to do this when they were at school, operating a fairly open house policy. I prefer to know where the children are as then I know they are safe.

The task of maintaining a balance between keeping the children happy, and allowing Max his ordered life, is made more difficult since the children do not know that Max has AS and so needs his sanctuary and routine, but I also do not think that they would be able to grasp the problems associated with AS. It is a hard enough task for an adult to understand let alone a child who has not yet understood their own emotional development. I also think that it could destroy, or at least damage, the wonderful relationship that they have developed with Max if they started to try to drastically alter the way they behaved around him. Max is far more tolerant of their misdemeanours than he is of those of adults, as he accepts that they are just children and adults should know better. He also does not want them to know, I think that this is in part because he still considers it as some type of mental issue, as do many people, and so does not want them thinking he is some kind of mental patient.

131

The three older boys have made comments about certain aspects of Max's behaviour and reactions to some situations, but none have ever indicated that they consider he has a problem, more that he is perhaps a little eccentric or slightly obsessive. One of them once asked if Max had Obsessive Compulsive Disorder and I just told him that he liked things in a certain way and he accepted that answer. I guess as Max's confidence grows, and he accepts his diagnosis realising that it is merely a difference in his approach to life rather than some sort of mental condition, he will be happier for the immediate family to be let in on the 'secret', but until then it will remain a secret.

My closest friend and confidant whose aunt is a head teacher at a school for children with Autism and AS asked me one day if Max had AS, and with a huge degree of trepidation I confirmed her suspicions. I felt I was breaking Max's trust but knew that she would realise if I lied. I asked her what had made her suspicious, because she had only met him a couple of times and usually he can hide it well in short bursts. It turned out, that little things I had said innocently about things we had done and funny occurrences had given it away, and her aunt had also noticed a slight awkwardness in him when he had been in a large group of people, and recognised the trait. It was quite a relief to be able to talk to someone who I could trust totally and have known since my childhood, plus I have the added bonus of her aunt's expert knowledge of the condition. I had to tell Max and this was extremely hard as I was worried that he would feel I had in some way betrayed him, but he was wonderful about it and could see that it would be very helpful for me to have someone to talk to. He never ceases to amaze me this is why I love him so much.

Interestingly he is quite happy for everyone to know that he has diabetes, yet refuses to tell anyone about the AS which is a shame. I understand that he doesn't want just anyone knowing about it, but if his boss was aware he wouldn't have half the problems at work that he does. Once they were aware of his dyslexia they gave him a special computer with a voice recognition programme, allowing him to dictate rather than type documents, and a personal assistant who can do all his filing and other paperwork, all particularly difficult tasks for him.

Long before we became a couple Max mentioned to me that he was struggling with three months of travel claims. I asked him what the problem was, and he told me that he had to look in his diary to see where he went each day, transfer this to the paper mileage forms with the details of who he was visiting, calculate the mileage and put that on the form, and add in the return journey. He said it was taking him hours because he kept forgetting the details between looking in the diary and putting it onto the form, so I offered to pop over to help him. When I got there he showed me the form he had already done and told me it had taken him three hours, there were about twenty journeys listed on it. Over the next two hours I completed another twenty forms finishing the mileage claim for him. The relief was immense as they would have taken him hours and caused him a huge amount of stress, although the exact level of this stress I would only find out years later, when I found out more about him and AS.

Now his personal assistant does the travel claim which is kept up together and submitted monthly; before his personal assistant, the forms would be submitted infrequently if at all because he would procrastinate, as he knew what a difficult task it was for him, but the longer he left it the worse it got because it just kept increasing. I can't begin to estimate how much money he has lost by not submitting the forms, but I understand that to him, the money was insignificant compared to the distress the form filling caused him.

I am sure that if he could just bring himself to admit to the AS in this day and age of equal opportunities and the disabilities act, there would be much more made available to him to help reduce his stress levels, and so reduce the likelihood of his depression continuing or getting worse. Hopefully this book will go some way to helping him accept and acknowledge the condition and become more open about it.

One incident which happened really early on in our relationship and almost destroyed it was our first holiday with the three youngest children; they were at that time seven, ten and thirteen years old. We took them to Spain for a week and stayed in a static caravan in a holiday village on the coast. The first couple of days were difficult but I thought we coped. Max found it really hard to cope with the children's demands and me allowing them to get away with things. I just wanted them to be happy and cause as little trouble as possible, as I knew Max would find this new situation hard enough to cope with without them being naughty.

What I didn't realise was that whilst I was focussing so much attention on the children, trying to stop them annoying Max and destroying our relationship, I was ignoring him. Max suggested that we should go to the camp disco one night. The two older boys said they wanted to stay in the caravan and watch some videos, the little girl, Charlotte, wanted to come with us; I said that this would be ok, not wanting to leave her with the boys as I thought they might argue, and we set off. We arrived to find a lot of families enjoying the evening. We ordered drinks and started to chat. Charlotte was dominating the conversation and demanding attention, which I was trying to manage along with focus on Max and his need for a relaxed and social evening. On several occasions he tried to divert my attention away from Charlotte, but I was too focussed on stopping her from playing up, that I didn't stop to consider his feelings. He asked me to get up and dance leaving Charlotte at the table, which I did not feel comfortable with, so I declined. Max got up on his own and started to dance in a provocative way trying to entice me onto the dance floor, Charlotte was making comments and wouldn't allow me to join him, which I know sounds very silly, but I was now in a real dilemma and unsure which way to proceed.

I didn't have to wait too long for a decision as Max made it for me; he suddenly returned to the table very angry and shouted that he should never have come on the holiday with us and that he was going home.

At that point I really thought that we were finished. I was mortified as I watched him head off into the distance. Charlotte was really shaken by the whole incident, so I tried to reassure her and we headed back to the caravan. I found Max sitting on the terrace outside so walked past him and put Charlotte to bed then returned to try and talk to him; he was not at all receptive so I went for a walk.

I sat on a swing in the children's park and just cried. Suddenly a group of French teenagers who were quite drunk appeared and became fascinated by my predicament. I was in no mood for company and tried to ignore their comments, they obviously thought I couldn't understand them so tried speaking a variety of languages including English. They were very intimidating and so I

135

ignored them as long as I could, and then, when they persisted, told them in French to stop being so rude and go away, just as I was doing this a security guard appeared and shooed them off, he asked if I was ok and I said, "Yes", but decided to go back to the safety of the caravan at that point.

Max was still outside, I sat down with him and we started to talk, he could see I had been crying and this is how the conversation started, as he didn't understand why I had been crying. We sat for several hours having a very difficult conversation, during which he pointed out my short falls, in particular the fact that I had ignored him the whole time making him feel isolated and not part of the family. He said that I was allowing the children to dominate me dictating everything and I just allowed it to happen. He didn't like the way they spoke to me either, he said it was very disrespectful and couldn't understand why I put up with it. He hadn't stepped in as he didn't think it was his place, but if I allowed it to continue then he would have to say something, otherwise we would be finished.

I just sat there totally numb. I really hadn't seen that I had been guilty of what he was saying, and it certainly had not been my intention to leave him out, on the contrary I had wanted him to see a lovely group of children who he could accept, and enjoy their company.

What he said was true, I had been focussed on them but not for the reasons he thought; when said it in the cold light of day, I saw that I did allow them to dominate and dictate to me, but this had been something they had done for years and I had misguidedly thought that by giving in to all their demands, I was being a generous and loving mother. It was really hard listening to these cold truths, but vital if our relationship was going to succeed. I agreed to try and change my approach, and asked him to tell me if I was focussing too much on the children's demands and not on his. I also told him that if he felt that the children were taking advantage of me then he should tell them. This cleared the air a bit so we went to bed, my head was swimming with guilt and upset.

The next day I drove us to Barcelona where we spent an interesting and useful day. Max started to take a more active role with the children, the first time I noticed this was when Edward, the eldest, decided he didn't want to eat what we were all eating because he wanted a Mac Donald's. If I had been on my own I would probably have given in because I wouldn't have wanted him to go hungry, Max told him that he should find something off the extensive menu or go hungry. It worked and he chose a pizza. Later he saw a large red truck with ladders and hoses on it and asked me what it was! I started to answer his question when Max checked me and told him to use his imagination.

This was a real eye opener, as I suddenly realised that I was constantly being asked stupid questions and answering them, rather than getting the children to think for themselves. No wonder I was always exhausted my brain never had a chance to relax.

Max and I walked hand in hand for the first time because up until then the children had always pushed in, this time I told them that we would like to be able to walk together. It was a much better day and I wasn't as worried about them as I had been. It was also nice for the first time in my life to have some backup and support.

On the way back from Barcelona we stopped at a small town to have some dinner. We had been there a few days before and noticed a roadside market. We told the children that they could buy some gifts to take home. We sat down at the table and ordered our food. They were quite busy so we had to wait some time. Whilst we were waiting Edward started asking about buying a BB gun. I explained that he was too young and said I didn't want to hear any more about it. A few minutes later Max and I were talking to Charlotte when Edward, who had been plotting with Patrick to think of new ways to try and get a BB gun, tried to get my attention. I ignored him until he suddenly clicked his fingers and shouted 'Mum'. This was the last straw for Max. He rounded on Edward and told him loudly, and in no uncertain terms, that he should never talk to his mother in that fashion as it was totally disrespectful, and if he ever did it again there would be consequences. Edward was very shocked, stood up and told Max that he wasn't his father then walked off. After a few seconds Patrick stood up and asked if he should follow him and we agreed. It was the first time that anyone had ever defended me and I was amazed and grateful.

Interestingly Max suddenly started to question whether he had spoken out of turn, and was worried that I would be upset over the incident, but I assured him he had not. This was the start of Max's parenting experience, thrown in at the deep end, a baptism of fire. In hindsight, a very dangerous thing, we should never have gone on such a holiday as a family so early on in our relationship, none of us were ready for such an experience, least of all Max. He was thrown into total turmoil trying to make sense of all the confusion, and the fact that he was not the centre of my attention, which I now know must have caused him extreme pain.

This was the starting point for our family building.

Over the last few years Max has been consistent in his approach to the children, and has always ensured that they do not disrespect me in any way. All decisions about the family are taken jointly after much discussion and we both support each other totally. It feels wonderful to have all this support and the children have responded well to this new found stability. They no longer have a mother who just gives in to keep the peace and they respect me for that. It is all down to Max's rules and moral codes, he is consistent in everything and the children know where they stand at all times. As a result they respect his decisions and have formed very strong bonds with him. I am sure that a lot of this insistence on rules and routines and following them through to the letter is part of his Asperger's, because many step fathers that I know, only play a small part in their step children's upbringing and discipline whereas Max is fully involved.

Christmas.

Every year as an adult Max used to get the usual gifts which had required very little thought such as socks, usually the wrong colour, he only ever bought black because they were less confusing when trying to pair them up after washing, and he always had an adequate supply of them, or toiletries which were useless to Max as he has very sensitive skin and can only use certain products.

About seven years ago he had an epiphany and realised that no one would ever buy him what he wanted, so he decided to buy his own presents. He had great fun searching the shops for presents that he really wanted; he then wrapped them up, put them under the tree and didn't touch them until Christmas day. It was his best Christmas ever; he spent it on his own with his tree, Christmas decorations and presents. He opened them gradually throughout the day thus extending his excitement with each new discovery. *"It never occurred to me before that, I spent hours buying presents for others. I had always loved Christmas and never looked back after that epiphany it was my best adult Christmas ever"*.

This obsession has been a lifelong thing unlike many of his other obsessions this has a prolonged focus. When he was quite young he watched a cartoon version of Scrooge and loved it, he spent years searching for it and eventually found it on the internet. It was an English made film which had been transported to America and not continued in England, if it hadn't been for the internet and his persistence he would never have found it.

Every year we start watching his vast collection of Christmas films on the 1st of December, and trawl the shops for new ones, it is a truly magical time, the most enormous tree is put up that night, and the room is transformed into a magical wonderland of lights and sparkly decorations; the children adore it and it is far better than any Santa's grotto or shop display even on our budget. Most of the decorations have been collected over the years and we try and add to them annually. We have great fun looking around the shops and markets for new shiny baubles to adorn the tree and living room, the only room we decorate. In the weeks after Christmas we look for sale bargains which we store for the following Christmas this also helps to extend the Christmas fun. This obsession certainly is one I would recommend to everyone.

The first Christmas I spent with Max was truly the best since my childhood it was filled with wonderful cosy childhood memories, anticipation and the excitement had been rekindled. Now I really look forward to Christmas with a renewed childlike glee.

One word of warning if your partner has the same childlike love of Christmas then you will probably have to find creative hiding places for presents. Max will rummage for hours if he thinks that I have bought him a present and hidden it. If I come home from a pre-Christmas shopping trip, I have to time it so that he is not home or leave the things in the car until he is not around. He will also question constantly, *"have you bought me a present yet, what is it, where is it, is it a ....?"* He will try as many combinations of questioning techniques as he can muster to try and break me down. I tell him that I wouldn't tell him even if I had bought him something, but this usually doesn't work as he knows that I will have spent a long time choosing a present, and finding a suitably sneaky hiding place. Some presents are incredibly difficult to hide due to their size so my creativity is pushed to the limits. I will not disclose successful hiding places as he is helping write this so reads it frequently, you will just have to use your imagination!

Max is also like this with the children, but they have been warned and they are getting very good at hiding things and not being drawn into his in depth mind games, even when they become devious! One day he told our daughter that if she loved him she would tell him what she had got him for Christmas! She wouldn't budge one bit and in the end he really loved his surprise present.

Another difficulty with presents for Max is that he has a knack for working out what is in a wrapped present. He will feel it, shake it, and listen to any sound it makes, then ask, *"Is it a...?"*, hoping that one of us will 'crack' under the pressure of his constant questioning, he is just like a child in this matter. You have to hold your nerve even

141

when he does guess correctly. I will refuse to give him the satisfaction of having been so smart. One way around this is to get creative with the wrapping, by trying to disguise presents in larger boxes, or putting two presents together both wrapped individually then wrapped again together to make an unusual shape. Or if he gets too good then I just don't put anything out until Christmas day. The children and I have done all of these and more, it has become quite a game which everyone enters into good naturedly, but it can become frustrating when you want him to have a lovely surprise and he keeps trying to sabotage it.

One of the best presents I ever got him was such a simple one, but it characterised his love of Christmas and is on permanent display over our bed. It is one of the bells off the reins on Santa's sleigh. For clarification watch the film 'The Polar Express' one of Max's favourites. He was so overjoyed with it, fascinated at how I had managed to find it, and really appreciative of the fact I had put so much effort into finding such a personal present.

Chapter14

Brutal honesty

Max agrees with this heading and says it is accurate in as much as he will always tell the truth, especially when asked a direct question, why waste time talking around the subject, just get straight to the point. Tact and diplomacy are not words in his vocabulary. One example that he finds hard to see as being in anyway wrong, was a comment he made several years ago at a family wedding. He spotted a woman with rather large hips and told her that she had *"good childbearing hips"*, Needless to say this was not taken as a compliment and the lady was very offended. Max couldn't understand what all the fuss was about; he had thought she would be very pleased to hear this, as he had seen a programme on television which said that women with large hips found it easier to give birth. Logically it would be far nicer to have an easy birth, so if your hips were wide you were very lucky!

The question 'does my bum look big in this?' also makes no sense to him. He can see no sense in a woman asking the question if she doesn't want an honest answer. If you are wearing clothes that you think make your bum look big, why ask the question already suspecting the answer to be yes, and then be upset when that is the reply. It is totally illogical.

I really appreciate his honesty because I know it is not said to placate me, it is exactly what he thinks and I am used to the bluntness of it, I accept that he sees no point in flowering information up and will give an exact answer. When we have talked about this Max has said that as a small child his mother told him it was important to always tell the truth, and he has therefore 'set' this as his default.

It is fixed in his head and therefore cannot be changed. Imagine the dilemma when he is then expected to compromise this rule and tell someone that their bum looks nice in a dress, when in fact it does look big, just because she might be upset with the truth, *"Why ask if she didn't want to know the truth. Does she really want to go out in a dress that makes her bum look big? Also there are so many contradictions, you should always tell the truth but sometimes you shouldn't. How do you know when these 'sometimes' are, what makes a situation, an always tell the truth situation and at other times, a don't tell the truth situation?"* The confusion it causes someone with Asperger's is immense as the whole thing seems totally illogical. This is just one of the daily dilemmas that an Asperger's sufferer struggles with, trying to make sense of the totally confusing non-Asperger's world.

Telling lies is not easy for a person with Asperger's,
"...if you are looking for an easy way to navigate and negotiate your way through the NT world of social gaming, forget it, there isn't one for Aspergians, so get real. It will always be a minefield. A college tutor asked me once; 'What's the best things to teach young Aspergians so they will be able to get on in the world?' After a pause for thought, I said; 'Well, if you teach them to lie and cheat, and generally misdirect people in everything that they say, treat others like shit, bully and constantly undermine and wind people up, and be a homicidal psychotic paranoid egomaniac. Be petty minded, overly bothered in other people's affairs and try to get away with as much in life as you possibly can, oh and don't forget the overall "blag" to be the person you are not...then maybe...just maybe they might stand a chance...but let's bear in mind...this is the NT world we're talking about... NT's learn how to lie comprehensively by the time they are four years old..."

Cornish from the book Asperger Syndrome & Social Relationships. Genevieve Edmonds and Luke Beardon 2008

They do not understand the subtleties, the social niceties and etiquette involved in avoiding upsetting people's feelings. They see everything in black and white so if asked the question, "Does my bum look big in this?", if it did, they would naturally tell her as they would expect she had asked because she wanted a truthful answer. I find this brutal honesty quite refreshing when looking for clothes and not wanting to go out looking like mutton dressed as lamb. Max knows exactly what he likes to see me in and what suits me and flatters my figure and age. He treats me to clothes when we spot something that he thinks I will look good in. I also enjoy looking good for Max and making him proud of me. I know when I go out I look good, because he would not allow me to go out looking dreadful. When I get a compliment from him I know that it is 100% honest. Beware of asking questions that you may not want to hear an honest answer to! It can sometimes bruise your self-esteem. The Asperger's sufferer is unable to put themselves into the mind of others and see things from their perspective. Everything to them is black and white.

What is generally true is that people with Asperger's can be very blunt and over-truthful when expressing themselves. In other words they are more likely to tell you exactly how they feel about how you look, or how a meal tastes, rather than shroud their feelings with the civility of a little white lie. They don't pick up the skill of polite refrain naturally, which is one reason they are considered to have poor social behaviour. Seems a contradiction, I know.

Max was asked many years ago by his brother Sean, who considered himself an artist, what he thought of his work which was plastered all around the room. Max was not impressed with it at all and felt that most of it was poor copies of other peoples work or very immature, so he told him he would rather not say, because he knew Sean would not be happy with the truth and Max wouldn't make up untruths. His brother kept on pushing Max for an answer asking him to tell him what he thought he said he wanted to know the truth. Eventually Max told Sean exactly what he thought of each piece. *"That looks like something a five year old would paint, that is a copy, no idea what you are trying to say in that one, this has no meaning at all."* and similar comments. This resulted in a huge argument, Sean was so upset by Max's comments that he resorted to hitting Max in the face and they didn't talk for years. Max says, *"It's not fair, why do people ask you to do these things and then hate you when you do?"*

"Because they're so *honest*, many people believe people with Asperger's can't lie, but most can certainly learn how to lie, even if they do it poorly. Those who are very rigid and rule-oriented may have a difficult time lying-- it may cause more anxiety than telling the truth-- but others with Asperger's can actually get very adept at lying, with practice". **(From the Autism: Support Group)**

Max can, *"bulls**t"*, his way through anything as long as he knows the rules. He was on a counselling course and Max decided to tell the tutor what she was going to do next. She took offense at this and asked, I think sarcastically, if he would like to debrief the course. Of course he took this literally as he didn't recognise the comment as being sarcasm, and did! I am sure he did a fantastic and professional job. The tutor got really upset and burst into tears asking Max to apologise. Max naturally refused because she had told him to take the debrief and that is exactly what he had done. He said, "*I will not apologise for doing what you asked me to do, but I am sorry if I have upset you*".

Max often gets into trouble when he goes on courses because of his literal thinking and his logic. When he arrived for a course on drugs, the first one he had ever done, they were presented with a selection of drugs and asked to name and classify them. Max refused to do it; when this was challenged, he told them that he wouldn't do it because he had come on the course to learn about different types of drugs, their street and generic names and their classification. It was pointless taking a test on a subject he knew nothing about, unless the object was to make everyone look stupid.

Often at meetings Max will listen to a discussion and then throw in a controversial statement which will open up a whole new avenue for discussion. This is not done to deliberately disrupt the meeting, it is just because he has been thinking laterally, is prepared to voice an opinion which others have probably been thinking but are too afraid to voice, or there is an inconsistency in the information being delivered.

"Hans Asperger (1979) had a very positive attitude towards those who have the syndrome and wrote: 'It seems that for success in science or art, a dash of autism is essential. For success, the necessary ingredients may be an ability to turn away from the everyday world, from the simply practical, an ability to re-think a subject with originality so as to create in new untrodden ways, with all abilities canalised into the one speciality". Tony Attwood Asperger's Syndrome A guide for parents and professionals.

Max is excellent at delivering ad hoc speeches or lectures if he has the knowledge base. Two occasions spring to mind, the first is when he was at a large multi-agency meeting, at which one of his senior bosses was meant to be delivering a speech; she was suddenly taken ill just before she was about to speak, and they needed someone to fill her place so asked Max if he would do it. He was very knowledgeable about the subject matter, so without any preparation stood up and kept the audience enthralled for the allotted time slot. When he returned and told me I asked him if he had felt nervous or conscious that he was not the expected speaker. He said, *"Why would I feel nervous I was just talking about things that I deal with everyday most of the facts and information she would have been saying I had just researched so it was easy. The people just listened to the facts and asked me questions"*.

The second occasion was his speech at our wedding. My eldest son had written a wonderful speech quite a while before the big day and asked Max how he was getting on with his. Max told him that he didn't need to write it out he would just 'wing it'. On the day, his speech was wonderful, no repetitions or hesitation, he remembered to thank everyone who had helped us, he was really animated and kept all of us amused with his anecdotes and jokes.

It never ceases to amaze me that he has no nerves when in front of large groups considering his dislike of social gatherings; he really should be on the stage as he can keep people riveted with his seemingly relaxed banter.

Another point to remember is that if you ask a question you will get a specific, precise answer with no elaboration. Max is getting better, if I raise my eyebrows when he finishes or say "and" he will add a little more. Most people will sense an underlying question, or get a feeling when a

148

question is asked, that more than a one word answer is required and adapt their answer to fit the emotional need of the person. Max will only answer the question asked and not acknowledge or notice any underlying agendas.

Max is very precise with his use of words. If someone uses a word incorrectly, either the actual word or the use of it Max will correct them. Max will usually have understood what the person meant but he still has to correct it. It is on occasion quite frustrating as I know he has understood and I will say, "You know what I/ they meant". His vocabulary is extensive and at times surprising. He enjoys the sound of certain words, and newly learnt words will be fitted into a conversation when possible, but always correctly.

He is a very private person and does not want people knowing his business. When I first started to meet his sisters, and started telling them that he had bought me flowers they were amazed and almost didn't believe me, questioning whether it was their brother I was talking about. He would shy away from sharing our personal information. With time he has realised that I only tell them because I am so happy with what he does, and want to 'show him off'. Many of my friends are jealous of all the romantic and caring things Max does for me, and the fun that we have. This is quite funny because they have no idea of the problems we have on a day to day basis, plus their understanding of his romantic gestures, is nowhere close to the logical and learnt thought behind his gifts and actions.

Chapter 15

Commitments and sexual relationships

Insecurity

Max needs constant reassurance where our relationship is concerned. He doesn't think that he is any good at being a husband. I constantly have to reassure him describing things that he has done which make me happy. He knows he has difficulties with the 'emotional stuff' and telling me that he loves me, so worries that I don't think he does. I explain often that it's the little things that he does every day that show me how much he loves me, flowers, chocolates, kisses, words of appreciation and practical demonstrations such as a cup of coffee.

I once asked Max to "never leave me", he said he couldn't do that as who knew what the future held. Very logical! Interestingly now Max often says *"Don't leave me"*. This is countered with, *"I trust you totally but if you ever betray that trust that will be the end of us"*. There would be no going back for him.

Max has a very low opinion of himself and when he has had a few drinks he often says, *"I am a twat."* I counter this by saying then, "I love and married a twat". He says this isn't true because that would imply that I was stupid which he knows a I am not, he is constantly telling me that I am one of the most intelligent people he knows and this was one of my initial attractions for him. It is very difficult when he gets like this because he cannot really define what he means, but I think he feels he is so different from other people in the way he behaves and understands the world, that it makes our relationship very hard. I on the other hand love him unconditionally and fell for his charms because of his innocence and gentleness. The quirks just make him more exciting. Life would be very boring if everyone were the same and conformed.

Max once told me he would commit suicide if I ever left him. He said this when he was very drunk and showing vast amounts of emotion, crying (first and last time I have ever seen this) and being very negative about himself. He said he was so frustrated that he was such a 'twat' and hated himself that our sex life was so bad. He told me that he lay awake every night angry at himself because he couldn't get aroused. This thought makes me feel terrible, because if I hadn't made it obvious that I really enjoyed our sex life he might not feel so bad about himself. It doesn't matter how many times I tell him that it doesn't matter, he still feels terrible about it. He feels inadequate as he is not fulfilling some kind of marital requirement. This I feel in part is a result of learnt behaviour from TV and films where sex demonstrates love and vice versa. I knew about this condition long before I married him yet he gets really upset about it which I think, in itself, stops the arousal, a vicious circle.

I try to make sure that I show how much I appreciate everything that Max does for me, as he often worries that he is not doing enough for me, and that our relationship is very one sided, I give and he takes. This is not true at all, but he needs to be reassured and I must demonstrate that I am happy. It was very difficult at first as a simple smile was not always recognised, but it has got a lot easier. I think that this should happen in all relationships because if you feel valued and appreciated then you give so much more back. Too often things are taken for granted over time and resentment sets in. Saying thank you for a cup of coffee is so easy, but over time couples forget to say it, making the gesture seem expected and not thoughtful.

He has no idea why he has low self-esteem, but he thinks it may in part be because he knows he has incredible thoughts and ideas, but a terrible memory. He can talk to people about new ideas, but has such a poor memory that he can't discuss details such as names of a new product or specific facts and figures, this makes him feel stupid. He loves listening to other people's ideas and says, "*Even the bad ones that I completely disagree with, I like to discuss them even if they are rubbish. They must be prepared to take criticism, intellectual discourse.*" I am also sure that years of bullying and being treated like an idiot, coupled with his feelings of inadequacy as a man and husband, have not helped in any way.

These feelings of inadequacy are voiced when Max has had a few drinks, the following are typical of the comments he makes, "*What saddens me is that I am not like this when I am sober. I have to continuously calculate thousands of things in my head all the time, so I can't show you how much I love you because I am not able to shut those other things out. Bacardi gives me the ability to love you, to see you for what you are, so loving, patient and tolerant, it shuts out all the other noise from the constant calculations in my head, I can focus on you and treat you as I should. How dare I tell you how much I love you when I am pissed and not be able to tell you when I am sober, it's a shame on you, its disrespectful and you know how important respect is to me. I am ashamed that I can't respect you when I am sober, I don't think you realise how bad it makes me feel. I have tried so hard to do the right things for you, I try to integrate with people but I open my mouth and a sentence comes out then the person answers me, but their sentence makes no sense to me and I fail you again. I so want the snuggle thing that you have but I can't have it, I don't feel it and I know that disrespects you*". It is impossible to reassure him. It is true that he is far more physically demonstrative when he has a few drinks, we kiss more passionately and more frequently, he will allow me to sit on his lap, he talks about intimate things and certainly in that way he fulfils his version of the perfect husband. What he will not accept is that when he is sober he is a wonderful husband, he is caring and protective of me, treats me with complete respect, we share chores, he appreciates everything I do, he constantly buys me little gifts showing me that he is thinking about me and much more. No matter how many times I tell him, whether he is sober or drunk he will not believe it, it is a completely impossible situation. I love him so much, but he is unable to believe me because he feels that he is not good enough, and it saddens me to hear him talking like this as he is so wonderful.

We talk openly and honestly about everything but I rarely, if ever, tell him if I am feeling down or ill. He does not handle this very well. He expects me to be happy, jolly and upbeat all of the time. This is very hard, everyone gets off days when they feel low, but I have to try and cover this up otherwise he gets down. If I have a 'sad' face he questions me constantly, *"Are you sad?"* *"What is wrong?"* etc. I have noticed that often I *"look sad"* as he calls it when I am concentrating on something. I know when I am sad and so make a concerted effort not to demonstrate it, because it has a really detrimental effect on Max. His mood changes and he worries which results in him getting low. He feels he has done something to upset me or is not doing something to make me happy, this is of course not the case but he automatically defaults to this assumption.

When Max is happy and relaxed with no stress he is a different person, his insecurities disappear and he is openly loving and demonstrative, put any stress or difficulties in front of him such as new people to meet, strange locations etc and he becomes anxious, looses confidence and withdraws into his 'bubble'. He makes a good job of hiding it but I know he is finding it difficult. Things have got easier over time, the more we venture out and have a good time the more relaxed he is the next time. He knows that I am there to 'save' him if things get too overwhelming and will get him out of the perceived 'trouble'.

It took me ages to realise that if he didn't understand something that I was trying to explain, it was because I was not explaining it in words that he could understand. I do not mean the actual words, it is more putting it into a context that he could relate to. It was quite frustrating at first but gradually I began to develop ways to explain things in Max speak! An example of this is when I tried to explain that sex was not the most important thing in our relationship. It was being happy and together that mattered and sex was an extra. He took it as a critical comment about our physical relationship, I had meant that our relationship was founded on far stronger things than sex and if we never had sex again, we would still be together and very happy as we had so much more. I also tried the medical route, that if one of us had an accident and were physically unable to have sex then we wouldn't split up, and when we are older and the desires decrease it wouldn't affect how we feel about each other. It took weeks to help him understand what I was trying to say, and even now I feel that there is still an element of disbelief concerning my motives and the statement. I had hoped that if I took that pressure or worry away from him he would feel happier but it backfired on me. It is so frustrating and takes a lot of thought to word things correctly, I now think before I say anything important so as not to be misunderstood or misinterpreted.

The fact that our relationship has survived this long indicates that it is very strong and nothing will break it. During the short time we have been together we have moved in together, survived being financially crippled, I have lost my job and Max's is hanging in the balance, we have coped with each other's idiosyncrasies, plus Max has had to adapt to not just one person invading his safe little bubble but also two young children on a permanent basis, and three older ones who drop in randomly. Not good for someone who doesn't cope with change. His daily routine has had to change dramatically to accommodate the children's demands. Yet through it all we have laughed and talked. If the stress and disruption get too much for him he retreats to the bedroom and sleeps, his only safety bubble. This action is accepted by all and not questioned. The effort he puts into the relationship is unbelievable for someone with AS. Coping with the constant changes and disruption to daily routine is something that many AS sufferers would not be able to do. He obviously loves me and the children very much to step so far out of his comfort zone to make our relationship work. He feels very strongly about the children and has thanked me for giving him a family, there are times when I worry that all the pressures of this family will prove too much, especially as they get older and more demanding. Sleep is a wonderful thing but I hope that it is enough to weather all the pressures of family and daily life with its ups and downs, disagreements and difficulties. I think that the description and analogy that Chris and Gisela Slater-Walker use about sleep and describes Max perfectly

"...Chris seems to go to sleep to escape resolving those issues he finds difficult to deal with. The only thing that prevents him from sleeping is indigestion. In the early days, after one of these unresolved arguments, I would be stalking around the house becoming more cross, while

155

Chris would be upstairs sleeping like a baby. Chris's ability to fall asleep in any position, in almost any situation is quite remarkable and a friend has suggested that it is rather like a screen saver, which seems to me a perfect analogy."

Max does use sleep as an escape when things are confusing for him or he has had a really stressful day. He will sleep or at least doze and this helps him to start making sense of the problem. If Max disappears I know I can find him asleep and he is able to do this almost instantaneously regardless of the time of day, outside noises or pressing commitments. If he needs to sleep he will. It may take several days to resolve whatever is bothering him but the sleep helps, just like the screen saver described in the quote! Interestingly until recently Max had suffered much of his life with extreme acid problems, consuming huge amounts of antacid on a daily basis. This, thanks to a wonderful doctor, has become a thing of the past. He has been prescribed a medication which he takes daily and does not have any problems with acid now so is able to sleep longer as he doesn't have to get up for more antacids.

Maxine Aston in Asperger's in love talks about control in relationships.

"Control is as essential to adults with Asperger syndrome as air to breathe. Keeping control is the only way they feel they can survive in a complex world full of mixed emotions and inconsistent feelings, all of which are a complete mystery to them. They have to try and interpret a language they have no knowledge of; there are no guidebooks on the unspoken word. Given that seventy percent of communication is unspoken, the remaining thirty percent does not leave them with much information to get by on.

No one is to blame for this, not the AS person or the person who is living with them.....Control is usually an essential requirement for the AS adult to maintain his life and keep some order in it. If you can imagine living in a world that is confusing, complex and totally unpredictable, you will realise why some control is essential for the AS adult, who is constantly striving to survive in this confusing world with only half a bag of tools in his social skills lit. This causes stress and anxiety, so he tries to reduce this by bringing in rules and routines that he does not have to interpret or think about, he can just do them automatically. This is vital to relieve pressure and anxiety; it is as therapeutic to the AS adult as a back massage or a glass of wine. It is a good way of winding down without having to think, talk or analyse, just going through the motions in the same way, rarely making any changes to the schema."

I have not experienced Max being controlling as such, he likes to be in control of certain things for example the morning bath routine. He has a need to have fixed plans such as, we will have to leave the house at 'x' to pick up a friend at 'y' and be at the restaurant by 'z'. I have never felt he has deliberately tried to control me, although there are occasions when his behaviour suggests that he will be unhappy if I do not comply with his wishes. To clarify, he will say in a sorrowful voice, *"Oh you are not going to bed are you; I was hoping we could chat for a while"*. Yes this is a form of control as he knows I find it hard to resist his 'puppy dog' eyes and manner, but if I insist then that is the end of it. When we first started to go out we used to talk for hours at night about some very in depth issues regarding our relationship and how Asperger's influenced it, however, in the last year or so as we have got more relaxed with each other and I have found that when I have mentioned certain issues, if he doesn't want to address them he will put his fingers in his ears and say "*la, la, la*". This is his way of controlling what he has to talk about, this can be really frustrating as we didn't have a problem in the past; I think it may be partly because he knows that he doesn't have to be on his best behaviour anymore, and he knows that I will not push him when he is not in the mood to discuss something. I am hoping that it will resolve itself with time because we had some really interesting and open chats, which certainly helped us consolidate our relationship and understand better how each of us tick.

On the whole I think our excellent communication has perhaps alleviated any need to control, plus he trusts my judgement and leaves many decisions to me, this reduces his stress. I make phone calls to people in authority such as banks, or sit with him if they will only talk to the account holder. I do find it difficult sometimes having to do all the 'important' stuff such as banking (money matters), doctors' appointments and social arrangements. At times it frustrates me as I know he is able to do it but just doesn't enjoy it and procrastinates as long as possible. This is how he dealt with it before we got together. I do understand his problems, as usually these types of call involve listening to complex and detailed information; often he misses important details because he has become focussed on a particular word or phrase and is trying to make sense of it, so misses the next few sentences. This then means that the rest of the conversation, once he has refocused, is out of context and he has to keep asking them to explain things and as a result feels inadequate. I enjoy 'looking after' him and he is so appreciative, it works both ways; for many years I had nothing to do with any money matters so have learnt a lot about this aspect of married life, I get things sorted out quickly and efficiently which reduces Max's stress. The only time I think he consciously takes control is when I say something that he doesn't want to hear or discuss, at which point he will say, "*I don't want to talk about it*" or he puts his hands over his ears and hums. It is his way of blanking the issue and I know better than to pursue it at that moment. When he feels ready we will talk about it.

There are many things that Max finds hard to do such as organise things, for example planning social evenings involving friends. Often one of his work colleagues suggests to him that we meet up for an evening. He will come home and tell me that I must phone the colleague and sort out the details, time, place, dress code etc. They are his friends yet he feels unsure how to proceed. It is so easy for me to make a quick phone call and it is all sorted. It relieves all Max's stress and enables us to have a nice time, without him worrying that we have got the details wrong and turn up uninvited or incorrectly dressed. This may seem like a simple task and one that Max could have done himself, but to him there are so many factors involved that could go wrong. Although he may want to go, the pressure of the details can be so strong that it would be easier, safer, not to go. If he forgets to ask about a certain thing, or forgets a critical piece of information, he would find it hard to deal with so it is far easier for me to do it.

Chapter 16

Routines

"Routine appears to be imposed to make life predictable and to impose order, as novelty, chaos or uncertainty are intolerable. It also acts as a means of reducing anxiety. Thus the establishment of a routine ensures there is no opportunity for change." Tony Attwood *Asperger's Syndrome. A Guide for Parents and Professionals.*

When I first met Max he had very fixed routines such as his morning routine. Get up, sit in his chair, have a cigarette, make coffee, another cigarette, put the bath on, another coffee with a cigarette, get in the bath, shave, hair, cigarette and coffee then off to work leaving the house at 0830. If it is the weekend he sits in his chair for an hour to come too before he has his bath. Over time he has allowed a little change to his routine, this has been because of the children needing to be up and ready for school. This has taken a lot of effort from him because the move from a sensible and practical routine, to a slightly chaotic one is not easy for someone with Asperger's. Once a routine that works is found it is not easy to justify changing it. Max says that routine greatly reduces his stress.

At work Max has a fixed morning routine. When he gets into work he must have complete quiet to go through his emails with no interruptions. Anyone who interrupts him will be met with a vacant expression and complete disinterest, or he will tell them he will not talk to them until he has finished his emails. Anything said to him during this time is not heard, he literally cannot focus on the two things so blocks the conversation so he can finish the emails, verbal communication is pointless. Max knows that he has routines, some of which are stronger and more essential to his survival than others, however, Maxine Aston notes that this acceptance of the need for routine may not be acknowledged by everyone with AS.

"Considering the frequency of routines and rules amongst adults with Asperger syndrome it was initially surprising that sixty-five per cent in my study said they did not have any routines or fixed ways. What their NT partners said, though, was quite different when they talked about their partners' various routines." Maxine Aston 'Asperger's in Love'.

Routines are comforting; they are a way of keeping control in what, to a person with Asperger's, is a very, out of control and unpredictable world. Routines reduce stress and depression.

"In Lorna Wing's paper (1981), she remarked on the high incidence of depression or affective disorder in adults with Asperger Syndrome. Clinical experience has also confirmed there is a greater risk for depression, with up to 15 per cent of adults having had a period of depression (Tantam 1991) and the genuine risk of suicide (Wolff 1995). During early childhood the person may be less concerned about their differences to other children. Their life revolves around their family and the teacher, with social contact with others having limited value or interest. During adolescence they start to become more interested in socialising with others and become acutely aware of their difficulties. The least intellectually able child in the class can be socially skilled, a leader and a comedian; yet despite their intellectual ability, when the child with Asperger's syndrome tries to have friends, to be the centre of attention or tell jokes, they are excluded, teased or ridiculed. This is the most common cause of depression – wanting to be like others and to have friends, but not knowing how to succeed.

161

Thus the cause of the depression may be an understandable reaction to having Asperger's Syndrome, but in some cases there may be a biological predisposition. Research studies have suggested that here is a marginally greater incidence of depression or manic depression (bi-polar affective disorder) in families that have a child with autism or Asperger's (DeLong and Dwyer 1988)." Tony Attwood Asperger's Syndrome A Guide for Parents and Professionals.

Music Routines

Max really enjoys music and has an eclectic collection ranging from classical to the latest nightclub favourites; and with his iphone and well researched car stereo that is compatible with his iphone, logging into it as soon as he gets into the car gives him the freedom to enjoy his favourite music where ever he goes. Prior to his iphone he would buy one album a year, and this would be the only music he would listen to for the whole year until he bought a new one. We would go on a long car trip and the same songs would play over and over again. On some albums there would be a song which he didn't like so would just skip it so that he could move swiftly on to ones he enjoyed. He gets just as much enjoyment from each song, no matter how many times he has heard them, as he did the first time he heard it. Then there comes a point when he wants a change, usually after about a year, and he gets a new album and the same routine continues. The iphone has given him the chance to have all his favourite tunes from across the years in one place, he can access them in the car or at home, via his docking station, and he loves it. Music is one of his great comforts; when he is stressed he will spend hours listening to it and disappear into his bubble, immersed in the sounds and images that they conjure up.

Chapter 17

Relationships

"The partner is often flattered by the intensity of the other person's dedication to them and their qualities of reliability, honesty and fidelity... marriage partners who do not have the same personality and interests tend to be very nurturing and protective individuals who compensate for any difficulties with the social aspects of life." Tony Attwood. Asperger's Syndrome. A guide for Parents and Professionals.

Max has had quite a traumatic time when it comes to relationships and most of the problems have been as a direct result of his condition. His first sexual encounter happened when he was 13 with a 16 year old girl that he knew. Max wanted a cigarette and she said she would give him a cigarette for sex. Max wasn't particularly interested in the sex but wanted a fag. It was his first time and he said it was enjoyable, but he didn't orgasm and there was no emotional attachment. His Mum was happy when she found out about his 'girlfriend', and was pleased that Max was not gay because up until then he had shown no interest in girls at all. Max has never really felt the need for many relationships, and all the relationships he has had have been entered into because he enjoyed the ladies company, and not for any sexual reasons. It has been the women who have pushed the sexual side, at which point Max has either backed off or felt duty bound to oblige.

"The person with Asperger's Syndrome can be vulnerable to being the victim of sexual assault". Tony Attwood *"...has known several victims of rape with Asperger's Syndrome, both female and male, but to date, no offenders."*

163

On one occasion a lady friend who he had known for some time invited Max up for coffee, Max thought that would be a nice end to the evening, having a cup of coffee and a chat, until she locked the door behind them and threw the key out of the window. Max went into a blind panic and whilst the woman was fixing the drinks Max managed to pick the lock using a self-made skeleton key and escape. He calls it *"rape"* as he felt totally sexually violated. I am sure that this episode has left a huge scar in his memory; it took him 4 years and several drinks for him to feel comfortable enough to tell me about it. He said that he had wanted to tell me many times before, but just didn't know how to start talking about it, yet felt guilty because I had been so honest with him about my abusive relationships.

Hormonally he doesn't feel he was any different from any other teenagers. His Mum had always told him that he must respect girls and he understood that. His relationships only lasted a few weeks and this was through his own choice for whatever reason, he enjoyed them at the time but didn't need it anymore. His Mum never understood his need to be alone.

Max's last relationship lasted about 3 months; this was a long time for him. Whilst with the lady, he said he felt as if he was in a clamp, and whenever he talks about her he calls her *'The Clamp'*. He felt she came too close all the time, and at night she would put an arm or leg over him *"clamping"* him. He would lie there waiting for her to go to sleep so he could move and sleep himself. The first time they had sex he had the biggest migraine he had ever had, and it came on the instant they started. He couldn't cope with the close contact and the fact that, when he had been

164

out and came home to her, she had "*the look*" and he couldn't understand why. The look he describes is a miserable, cross one as if he had done something wrong. He knew that he had needed the time out and yet got this pressure when he went back, which was very confusing as he expected her to be pleased to see him.

It all ended when he had decided to spend some time away from her and go back to his house. She turned up and when Max answered the door, "*She was standing there with a miserable face*". It was at this point that he knew it was not going to work and he told her that it was over.

"*In all other relationships, I guess with hindsight, I just didn't have the emotional understanding. The only way to explain or understand it is by the Rolo incident, which ended up with the girl crying because I ate the last Rolo in the packet she had given me as a present. No-one explained it to me until afterwards. My life has been loads of faux pas's. How was I supposed to know that I was supposed to give the last Rolo to the girl if no-one told me?*"

"*I am not sure what love is. I understand from a logical point of view what it is. The problem is when people tell me about love and what they feel inside, I don't understand as I haven't experienced it and so don't know what they are talking about*".

Max went on to try and explain how he felt about me.

"*If you change the word from love to share then it becomes easier to understand. If there is a person who typifies this it would be you, because you allow me to be me, allowing me to push my boundaries. There is no-one else in the world that I could do this with*".

165

Sexual conversations.

Max and I enjoy going to our local nightclub and chatting to people there. We have made many friends over the last few years so our conversations sometimes have a cheeky element. If we arrive late one evening one of the chaps might say "what have you two been up to?" inferring that we have been making love. One night I had worn a dress that Max particularly liked me in, and he took great pride in 'showing me off', which prompted smutty comments about what we would get up to later on. Max played the game and followed the male type banter for a while. He does not enjoy it but knows that it is required to be socially accepted. It's a man thing I guess, very macho, egotistical, bragging that sort of thing and I play along where required. One night, one of them implied that if Max wasn't up to the job he would be willing to oblige, to which I replied, "I doubt you would come anywhere close to satisfying me the way Max does". In fact this was probably closer to the truth than they realised because it's not about the physical act, it is about the whole package, intimacy, conversation and closeness.

Size is a big issue with men and I have often remarked, during such smutty exchanges, that most men would find it hard to compete with Max in that department. I guess it is partly a protective thing, plus it boosts Max's ego, but it does leave me thinking occasionally how ironic such exchanges are. I wish I knew how to help Max change or overcome these sexual problems, because I know how much they bother him. What makes things easier is knowing that I am not alone in this, many couples where one has Asperger's Syndrome experience problems in their sexual relationships and many far worse than Max and I do. Some couples never consummate their relationship and others have major challenges with touch sensitivity.

Inheritance

"There are also some families with a history of children with Asperger's Syndrome and classic autism (Gillberg 1989, 1991; Gillberg, Gillberg and Staffenburg 1992). Thus a brother or sister of the child may be diagnosed as having autism, and further investigation of the family suggests a sibling with Asperger's Syndrome. There are also families with several children or generations with this Syndrome". Asperger's Syndrome. A Guide for Parents and Professionals.1998

Since Max has been discussing Asperger's with me, and as our understanding grows, we have noticed definite traits in one / two of his younger brothers. Max has five brothers and three sisters. We know nothing about his father, but Max had a wonderful mother who accepted each child as an individual and encouraged them all to be themselves. I think this helped him and his brothers, if we are correct, deal with their Asperger's within the home and to a degree outside. One of Max's brothers is very similar to Max he is solitary, rarely has relationships with women, and finds it very difficult to socialise with people even relatives; he relates to younger people far better than adults. The other brother is virtually a recluse no one in the family sees him and he only goes into town for essential shopping.

"Fragile sites have been identified on the X chromosome (Anneren et al 1995; Gillberg 1989) and chromosome 2 (Saliba and Griffiths 1990) and other chromosomal anomalies such as translocation have been associated with Asperger's Syndrome (Anneren et al 1995; Gilberg 1989). In particular, children with Fragile X syndrome, a

167

relatively common genetic abnormality, can develop characteristics consistent with Asperger's Syndrome". Asperger's Syndrome. A Guide for Parents and Professionals. Tony Attwood 1998

Flirting

Max is very attractive to other women, this may be because he has a boyish innocence and charm which is quite attractive to women. He doesn't come across as a man who is only after one thing, quite the opposite and this puts women at ease, and may present them with a challenge. It is unusual to find a man like Max, and once women find him attractive and flirt with him, they are surprised that he doesn't reciprocated and try and take it further. Before we started seeing each other I had watched such scenarios played out in front of me. Women from all walks of life, married, single, old and young flirted with him. None were successful he simply chatted and seemed oblivious to their attentions until it was actually stated, offered on a plate! He could take part in the banter and sexual innuendos and play the game, after all he had observed this time and time again on the TV and in films, and learnt it. I honestly don't think he realises they are serious; I think he thinks they are playing a game too. Communication through body language is completely different to spoken language, and the banter used when flirting, is accompanied with body language which goes over the top of Max's head. When I have explained such occurrences to him he is amazed and quite shocked, saying that he has had nothing to do with it and is innocent. I know this is correct as I have seen it happening so reassure him.

On one occasion before we were a couple, we were at a cadet training weekend and had had a large meal with lots of alcohol, everyone was very merry; three of us were talking when a man, who we knew from another area, approached and blatantly started flirting with Max. After several minutes I realised that Max was oblivious to what was going on so I jumped into action, grabbed his arm and said, "hands off, he's mine". It worked and Max wasn't bothered again. When I explained the reasons for my actions he was horrified, but commented that the man had always been very friendly in the past. He is not the first man to find Max attractive and I am sure he won't be the last. At least I am now around to protect him from any unwanted attention.

It is interesting that I do not feel threatened by the unrequited adoration and attraction that these women feel for him. I know that I am the only one that Max will ever commit to. It may sound daft but after all the years Max has been single, he has decided to commit to me because he doesn't want anyone else and never will. He says that if I ever leave him then there would be no one else, and he would retreat into his bubble and stay there.

I am also aware that if I ever broke Max's trust that would be the end of our relationship. I am a big flirt and enjoy the flattery and banter, Max is ok with this, however, if I ever over stepped the mark, there would be no going back we would be finished. We had a horrid moment one New Year, when a mutual friend who we had made when we first started courting, kissed me on the lips. It happened in a nightclub in the early hours of the morning New Year's Day. We had been laughing and joking for much of the evening and Max and I had been taking pictures of us with friends and acquaintances. This particular friend, Sam, had put his arm around my shoulder and we were posing for a photo. Just as Max was about to take the photo, Sam put his hand on my cheek and turned my face towards his, he

169

then kissed me. Whether he had intended to kiss me on the cheek or the lips is not clear; I was not really conscious of the full impact of his actions until we looked at the photos days later. Max saw them first and was horrified and furious; I was shocked and upset as I would never voluntarily have kissed him on the lips. We didn't really talk about it for a few days, as I knew Max was really distressed, and I was both angry at Sam and worried about Max and our relationship. I couldn't believe that this had happened, but obviously couldn't deny it because there was the evidence in front of me. Unbeknown to me, Max had been studying the photo in great detail and realised that Sam had pulled my face round, rather than me voluntarily kissing him. The matter was resolved and never spoken about again. You may think that the fact that Max checked the photos in detail might indicate that he didn't believe me I, however, know that he wanted to believe me, and the proof that I was innocent of the 'crime' lay in the photograph which he was able to see with his own eyes. Interestingly we have not seen Sam since and I certainly am pleased about this, as I felt violated, maybe this is too strong a word but certainly 'used', and he could have destroyed our relationship with his thoughtless act.

Faithfulness.

Faithfulness is of paramount importance to both of us. Max's high morals were first apparent when he made it clear that there would be no relationship between us until I had separated from my husband, and had been that way with divorce proceedings in place for a minimum of six months, even then he was concerned that this might not be the appropriate length of time and spent hours on the internet researching the correct time frame. I found this out later.

"A man with AS can be altruistic, helpful, and, at times, positively heroic. Yet, when he is "expected" to come through for someone, he may not be able to handle it. For example, one man refused to visit his aunt after she'd had a stroke though she asked for him daily (they were close, at least in her eyes). He wouldn't even admit to himself that she'd had a stroke or that she might not survive. It was busy season in his work and he didn't have time to spare, especially when he believed she'd be home again soon anyway. It can be hard to maintain respect for him in the face of such behaviour."
Rudy Simone 22 Things a woman must know if she loves a man with Asperger's Syndrome.

Max is very selfless and does things because he thinks it is the right thing to do and not for any accolade. He doesn't boast or talk about the things he does, it only comes to light in a roundabout way. He has had a back injury in the past which occasionally plays up, when I asked him how he had first injured himself, he told me that he had helped an old lady who had fallen over, and when he lifted her to her feet his back had started to play up, and he had to take a week off work. Since then periodically he has suffered pain.

Chapter 18

Sex

Many relationships have problems with their sexual relationships, regardless of whether one of the partners has Asperger's Syndrome or not, however, by nature, Asperger's Syndrome can add extra challenges to the successfulness of a sexual relationship. During sex many senses are highly stimulated, and this can cause extreme pain for the sufferer, as they have trouble dealing with more than one stimulus at a time.

This is a really difficult thing to talk about because it is very private and intimate, something that is usually kept between two people. When I started reading books about relationships between a non Asperger and someone with Asperger Syndrome, I was very disappointed to find that this one area which was causing us so much heartache, was not discussed candidly, in fact there was very little mention of it at all. It was brushed over with comments like;

"For us, fortunately, this part of our marriage is very happy, and unlike Marge and Homer Simpson we do not have the urge to make it public, so we are keeping this chapter short and discreet". Gisela and Christopher Slater-Walker. An Asperger Marriage.

or technical information about how there are problems with hypersensitivity and touch, or lack of sexual arousal. Max and I think we should discuss our problems not because we wish to worry couples in the early stages of a relationship, or upset those where there is no sexual activity, merely to offer an honest insight into our dilemmas, in the hope that others can see that regardless of problems encountered with the physical side of a sexual relationship, a real relationship is built on much stronger and deeper things.

Some of our problems may be related to the 'onset' of chronic depression. Max has suffered from bouts of depression for many years. About 18 months into our relationship Max was diagnosed with chronic depression, and it was about this time that our problems increased. I do not think that our relationship has been directly responsible for the longevity of the depression, but I do think it has a bearing. Depression is a recognised problem associated with Asperger's syndrome so may be a contributory factor to many similar relationships.

"Although depression was cited fairly frequently by AS men, fifteen per cent of them still felt the relationship was worth it compared to the loneliness they felt before. They discussed the longing they had felt to be accepted and needed. They felt that no matter how depressed they may feel now, it was far better than the way they felt when they were on their own and worried that they would never find a partner". Asperger's in Love. Maxine Aston 2003

In Max's case the depression started as a result of a major work overload which wasn't dealt with when initially voiced to his superiors, culminating in a three month sick leave and huge amounts of antidepressants. These were increased after a year when there was no marked improvement. I think that had we not been in a relationship the problems at work on their own would have been dealt with better by Max, as he could have come straight home and gone to bed without having to deal with anything else. If he still couldn't cope, he would have been signed out sick and his recovery would have been easier, because he would only have had to think of himself. I had noticed a definite decline in his sexual desire as his workload had increased, so wasn't surprised to hear the diagnosis, as I know that a symptom of depression is a reduction in sexual desire. I had realised that he was getting more and more stressed which also effects desire. After another six months of stability without improvement and several months of pestering the doctor, Max finally got a diagnosis of Type 2 diabetes which in itself can cause sexual problems so, although we had sexual problems before the diagnosis, the depression and diabetes has not helped. It is not completely clear how much is related to Asperger's alone. Max said that in his youth he 'dated' girls and had carnal thoughts and sex. He had never understood relationships and so was fearful of the intimacy involved in a long term relationship, so backed off before his relationships got to that point. He says, *"It is very difficult to describe this fear and lack of understanding of intimacy"*.

I know we shouldn't complain or worry about it since there are some relationships that have never been consummated, but it is something that really affects Max's mental wellbeing.

We have tried to get help from the doctors, as he is really conscious of the fact that he doesn't have a sexual drive, and if he does get aroused it often doesn't last very long. We were prescribed Viagra and were very hopeful that this would help the situation. It works on the basis that when you feel sexually aroused and find difficulty getting or maintaining an erection it will assist you. We have tried it on several occasions and at several stages of arousal and it has not made the slightest difference. It certainly doesn't work if you have no interest at all!

In order for a man to be able to control orgasm he has to

174

be aware of what is going on with his body. He needs to be in touch with the physical sensations he is feeling; it requires that mind and body be linked. If he is anxious or worried about his performance his mind will not be fully focussed on the bodily sensations that lead to orgasm. Asperger's in Love Maxine Aston

I think Max has this problem because he is very conscious that a man is normally able to have an orgasm inside a woman, and that healthy relationships usually contain some sexual activity. He has only ever ejaculated once inside a woman and that was me.

At the time he thought that I was cross about this, although he didn't say anything until months later when it came up in a conversation about our sex life. I am sure that this has had a direct impact on his ability to ejaculate ever since. He is convinced that I was not happy that he had come inside me, so now I think he is unable to for fear of upsetting me. Max is very conscious of the fact that he doesn't come and I think that the longer this goes on the worse it will get. I have told him on many occasions that I was not upset only surprised and, as we were just about to go out, I had to have a wash before we left the house.

"Retarded ejaculation is a difficulty in reaching an orgasm and can vary greatly in severity. The more severe it is the harder it is to put right. It is about having too much control and holding back. For some men it only happens while they are having intercourse, and they may find it possible to reach an orgasm while having oral sex or being manually stimulated by their Partner. Others may only be able to reach an orgasm through masturbation. Anxiety or inner conflict with the partner can cause retarded ejaculation. It can also be caused by anxiety over commitment issues with their partner; this type normally

175

manifests itself in an inability to ejaculate inside the woman...Anxiety and AS are often linked together. The AS man is constantly having to work harder at reading situations and trying to work out if he is getting it right. The more he focuses on this the less he will be focussing on what his own body is doing". Asperger's in Love Maxine Aston

When we were making love more frequently, once every one or two months or so, he would often lose the erection part way through particularly if we changed position or paused momentarily. Now he rarely gets aroused and is often not in the mood at all.

"Impotence, the inability to achieve an erection, was the problem most frequently mentioned by couples I spoke to who were experiencing sexual problems. For some of these couples there had been a complete abstinence from sex for many years, sometimes decades. Most of these women felt cheated, undesirable and frustrated, and most did not have any idea why their partners could not make love to them. Some of the answers to why this happened came from the AS men I spoke to. Many of these men said that they preferred masturbation to making love with their partners." Asperger's in Love Maxine Aston

We are working on this and I never suggest we try to make love, the idea has to be his otherwise he feels pressurised and nothing happens, and then he feels guilty because he knows I would like to make love and he isn't in the mood. It is a very upsetting position for both of us. We are intimate in other ways, chatting and cuddling occasionally but the physical side of our relationship seems lost at the moment. We have not given up and hope that once we have the depression and diabetes under control things will improve again. There are occasions when I feel undesirable and wonder what I am doing wrong to make me so unattractive sexually. I know this is irrational given the fact that many others, in similar relationships, experience the same thing, and that Max feels guilty about not getting sexually aroused; but it still doesn't stop me thinking it. I lie next to him willing him to turn over and make love to me, I know it isn't going to happen but I still hope.

There are a lot of good things about our sexual relationship. I have never felt so relaxed and comfortable with anyone before. Early on in our sexual relationship he explored my body complimenting me and caressing me and there was no embarrassment. It was as if he had never had the opportunity to really look at a woman's body, and was fascinated with the differences between men and women. He questioned things and asked if what he was doing felt nice, and asked what else he could do to make it more enjoyable, because of the way he is I did not feel self-conscious. When I told him what was pleasurable he was ready to try it because he wanted to make me feel good. Another wonderful thing is that we laughed constantly, it may sound odd but we could be in the middle of making love, and one of us would say something or move position, and this would make the other one laugh and then we were off. This helped keep the mood light and fun which eased any tension.

Even though the 'technical' side of our relationship has not been overly successful. I think that, although hugely important to Max and me, laughter, caressing and exploring is something that many non Asperger couples miss out on in their haste to satisfy their sexual needs. Regardless of our lack of actual sexual activity our bedtime relationship will always be a good one because of the closeness. My only sadness is that I know that Max goes to bed every night frustrated that he cannot get aroused enough to have sex, which is what he thinks is required as a husband to sustain a happy marriage. When we do make love it is a wonderful experience, one which I have never felt before, but it is not the main part of our relationship, it is the closeness every night when he kisses me and holds me close before turning over to go to sleep, massaging his back when he is stressed or can't sleep, rubbing his tummy, or talking about our future. These things constitute a far closer bond to me than the physical sexual act, enjoyable as it is. I have often said sex isn't everything, what if one of us was physically handicapped for example paralysed, it wouldn't stop us making love because this is about being close, touching, talking and enjoying each other's minds and bodies.

Chapter 19

Conclusion

The purpose of writing this book was to offer an insight into the difficulties and delights of a relationship between two people, one with Asperger's syndrome and one without, in the hope that it will encourage couples to work at the relationship and not fall at the first hurdle, as the benefits far outweigh the difficulties. There are parts of the book that might give the impression that it is virtually impossible for anyone to survive such a relationship, but I hope that I have countered this with the positives. All relationships require effort and compromise from both partners to succeed, and ours requires more than most, but I know that this 'work' is a small price to pay for the wonderful fun and closeness that we have.

Whether or not your partner has had a formal diagnosis you obviously suspect that they may have Asperger's Syndrome. The fact that you are reading this book indicates you have decided that you want your relationship to succeed. It is important for both of you, (if possible) to realise the problems which you might encounter along the way, and have some chance of finding strategies to help overcome them. I hope that we have gone some way to helping you with this. The Simon Baron-Cohen test at the end of the book may help your partner to better accept the diagnosis or your suspicions. Max found it very interesting.

By its very nature the world of the Asperger sufferer is confusing and stressful. They struggle to make sense of every day to day occurrence, juggling a thousand thoughts, sights and sounds in their heads, trying to make sense of all the seemingly illogical behaviour around them. To help them cope with this constant 'noise' we as the non Asperger partner must allow them time to de-stress by retreating into their 'cave'. This can take different forms depending on the individual. In Max's case sleep, computer time and music are his three main coping mechanisms, so when he retreats I 'allow' him the down time because a de-stressed Max is a happier and more affectionate Max. This makes me happy and when I am happy Max is happy.

I think if you can view the syndrome as a difference rather than a disorder, then it puts a more positive slant on it. People are labelled far too much, fitted into little boxes and expected to exhibit typical behaviour, however, Asperger's Syndrome, although it affects three main areas of daily life, the extent to which they are affected is hugely variable with each individual. They may have managed to learn to cope better in one area than another, or are hardly affected in some areas and worse in others. This can be confusing to the sufferer who is trying to make sense of the syndrome. When we started our research Max would identify with some problems and not with others, putting an element of doubt in the diagnosis, this is something which Asperger sufferers do not like, they are very logical and therefore do not like grey areas. It took a long time for him to realize that it was typical of the sufferer not to exhibit all the symptoms talked about in text books, and to have them in varying degrees. I think this is a point which must be empathized to avoid confusion and it has certainly helped Max through this process of self-discovery. '

We have found that our longstanding strong friendship and shared interests have seen us through tougher times, and it is important not to forget what attracted us to each other in the first place. I love his gentle nature, his calm and logical manner and his slightly quirky sense of humour.

Max loves my patience, the fact that he can talk to me and I appreciate his jokes. Even in the most stressful times we find things to laugh about and this sees us through. It is important for both partners to remember why they wanted to be a couple when things get tough.

Bullying is an issue which prevails amongst Asperger's sufferers and long term this affects how the sufferer regards other people and the world in general. Self-esteem and insecurity are huge problems, and directly affect the relationship. It is very important to remember that your partner needs constant reassurance from you; they need to know that what they are doing, even the simplest things like making you a coffee, is appreciated, so should be acknowledged; they must know that they have done the right thing. Constant reassurance is a key issue and one which doesn't always come easily when you are tired or busy, but it does pay dividends, he will feel so appreciated and reassured that he is doing the right thing. Low self-esteem leads to defensiveness which is often aimed at you, it is really difficult to deal with this when they have over reacted to a simple question, but it is important to remember at these times that they do not mean to upset you, the confusion in their head takes over and they react negatively as a self-preservation mechanism; after a little while they will manage to process the information and the matter will be resolved, just give them time and space.

Trust is something which needs to be earnt in any relationship, but it is far more difficult when one partner has Asperger's. For much of their life they have been lied to and they stop believing anything that is said to them, because they are unable to distinguish the truth from lies. They do not know why people lie they just know they do. Once an idea is so firmly fixed in their heads they cannot believe otherwise. To make your relationship work it is vital to demonstrate that you are trustworthy, idle chatter with friends can be viewed as an invasion of privacy and a betrayal of secrets that they shared in a trusting moment with you. These 'secrets' may not seem that important to you but to your partner they are, this should be remembered if you are to be trusted.

The other side of the coin is your trust in your partner. By their very nature, Asperger sufferers rarely elaborate on information, they deliver it in its simplest form which could be construed as secretive or evasive. It is important to remember this and work on ways of helping them to elaborate, this will not be easy for them, and it will take a lot of time and effort on both sides to start to improve it. I, for my part, do not push Max for constant elaboration as this would be too tiring for him, just on things which I feel are important, but each relationship is different and you have to decide what a happy medium is for both of you.

Communication in social situations is an area fraught with difficulties for Asperger's sufferers; but it is also probably the area in which you can be the most influential. It is a huge responsibility and not one to be undertaken lightly, as mistakes can leave a huge dent in your partner's confidence. They do not read body language or facial expressions well, so may come to rely on you to do the interpreting and pass the information on to them somehow, this simple 'code' is something that is developed over time alongside the relationship, partly because you are probably thrusting them into more social situations than they would have normally allowed, and partly because you can sense when they are getting stressed. It is important to respond to their confusion in these areas and be prepared to make excuses to leave the event early, if it is getting too stressful for your partner, without a fuss or scene. Do not use them as the excuse as this will undermine what little confidence they had in the first place, after all they probably only came with you because they wanted to make you happy. It is a slow process but it is worth the effort as we have found out. Max now goes out far more often than he ever did before and enjoys himself, despite the fact that he finds it immensely stressful at times. He is also able to give me little signals when he needs me to get him out of difficulty, which is a very useful skill to develop. Be their safety net and your social life should improve dramatically!

You need to be aware that they will always default to the literal which can cause problems in conversations with people, again you can help them out by intervening subtly when you sense they are about to get themselves into a difficult situation, or getting them out of it with a witty comment or a diversionary tactic.

Another issue with their communication abilities which can cause major problems between you is when it comes to discussing feelings. Their tendency to default to the literal, along with their need to analyse every possible meaning of a phrase or sentence and their poor ability to read body language and emotions, often leads them to draw incorrect and negative conclusions about personal things you have discussed. Their natural tendency to assume a negative stance will often result in your comment being seen as a criticism of them and their abilities. It is very difficult to convince them otherwise as they may have mulled the thought over for some time, and have a rigid idea in their head by the time they mention it to you. My advice is, try to word everything accurately, try not to say anything misleading or that could be misinterpreted. This is extremely difficult and takes a lot of thought and effort on your part. With time and good communication between the two of you it does get easier.

Max has accepted that occasionally he does misunderstand what I have said or have been trying to say, possibly in a clumsy way, we discuss it and clear the air. He will probably not believe me one hundred percent as he is convinced he is never wrong, but just the fact that we have discussed it helps.

Brutal honesty is a very difficult topic as it can not only be offensive to other people, but also hurtful for you. Other people may regard such comments as rude and unnecessary and chose not to associate with your partner again, that is their loss in my opinion, but it can still be rather embarrassing in social situations so you may have to develop a thick skin! When the comment is aimed at you it can be very hurtful. It is really important to remember that it is not a personal slight, merely a statement based on an observation. They do not mean it to be upsetting they were just stating a fact. It took me quite a long time to get used to this concept and you have to be strong, with Max, as our relationship has developed we have been able to talk about these incidences, usually sometime after the event, and he is more aware how hurtful they can appear and has tried to think before he comments. It is not fail safe but it does help. Try and work on discussing these issues, again not an easy task, and it may take some time for your partner to be open to discussing them, since they might view your suggestion that the comment was hurtful as a criticism, but worth working at and waiting for. It is also refreshing at times to know that if you ask your partner a question you will get an honest answer; very useful when you suspect that your outfit may not suit you as well as the sales assistant is suggesting!

Trying to convey important information without having your partner's full attention is a waste of time. This is a lesson that should be learnt very early on unless you want to be let down or disappointed, and I think that many partners learn this the hard way. If you need them to remember something or do something, then do not tell them when they are pre occupied. Make sure you have their full concentration and when necessary have a backup plan such as a timely text or a list. These memory jogs will ensure that they are not side-tracked by some outside influence or dilemma.

Obsessions are an interesting area and one which can present problems but they may also prove very useful. They can be difficult to cope with at first because, by their very nature, they can dominate every available waking hour leaving you feeling left out. Over time it is possible to come to a compromise much as you would with a child, 'four hours with your computer and then we go out for a walk', be prepared for the four hours to be extended a little while they finish some vital thing but it does work. It is logical and therefore can be rationalised. Looking at it from a positive view point, you are guaranteed a period of time to follow your own hobby or go out to visit friends, without worrying that your partner may be feeling neglected. Max will go on the computer and I can sit and read without feeling guilty that I am leaving him out whilst my head is buried in a book. If you can develop hobbies together then this can also be rewarding, but your partner will probably want to be in control and do it their way or not at all. Writing this book has been a joint effort and interestingly has become quite an obsession for me and merely an interest for Max, so he has felt able to pursue his own interest's knowing I am not going to ask him to stop, guilt free! I say guilt free, as he is aware that he disappears for hours at a time when he gets totally absorbed in something, and knows that I do, at times, find it hard; but I always remember that it helps him relax so when he reappears de-stressed we enjoy each other's company far more plus we have lots of things to talk about.

In normal relationships emotions and responses to them play a major part, however, in relationships where one party is unable to recognise and respond effectively to an emotion, problems are bound to arise. People with Asperger's, contrary to popular opinion, do experience emotions; however the problems occur when they have to recognise an emotion in another person and respond appropriately, in other words, empathise. They are unable to do this effectively and will often ignore the emotion or give an inappropriate response, which in itself can escalate the situation. It is very important that you realise this early on otherwise you will feel hurt, unloved and undervalued. It is important to remember that they are not deliberately being insensitive, in fact they are probably painfully aware that they are not responding to your emotional needs in the expected fashion, but are unable to work out what is required. Over time we have talked and Max knows that if I am sad he needs to give me a cuddle and say things like, 'everything will be ok' or 'I am here for you'. You need to explain exactly what you need as they will not instinctively know but they can learn. It is very hard at first as it feels quite unnatural explaining what you want someone to say or do in times of emotional distress as every situation is different, but it does get easier and once one or two simple phrases and actions are in place more can be added to suit different occasions. This may sound contrived but it really helps when you are feeling low, the response is learnt but it goes a long way to making you feel appreciated and understood. It also helps them to feel more in control of the situation and, rather than walking away from you when you appear upset, they will try to support you with practical demonstrations of affection and understanding. If you don't expect too much then you will be pleasantly surprised. Because they learn things from information gleaned from the TV, conversations or the internet they are able to recognise that partners enjoy receiving personalised cards and presents, so they may take a lot of time and effort searching for wonderfully interesting gifts for you, after all when you are happy so are they. Equally demonstrations of the same care in choosing the perfect gift for them is greatly appreciated, and goes a long way to proving that you do genuinely care for them helping to boost their self-esteem.

Love seems to be a hard concept for them to understand as it is an emotion that many normal people struggle with. There is no easy fix for this one, you are feeling and experiencing butterflies and euphoria, and they are just accepting that you are in their lives and are struggling to cope with someone invading their solitary world. What you must keep in mind is that, the fact they have allowed you this far is a huge step for them and a massive demonstration of their attempt to form a relationship, they have trusted you more than most people, and you should be honoured that they have seen something special in you, because it is not easy for them to allow people to get close.

Being a step dad is not easy for anyone but it is especially hard for someone with Asperger's. They are very self-centred and find it difficult to share. Having to share you with your children is very hard, add to that the fact that children tend to be self-centred as well, and this can be a recipe for disaster. You might find yourself stuck in the middle trying to keep both sides happy, especially if the children do not know about your partner's condition. There is no easy answer to this and a lot is dependent on the age of the children and whether you are living together or not. My advice would be to try and make time for you to be alone together. I am very lucky as the children have accepted Max relatively easily and he is wonderful with them. Patrick and Max enjoy the same type of humour and Charlotte is naturally very affectionate and giving, so this helps but not all relationships are as easy. You will have to do a certain degree of mediation, explaining to your partner that they are children and so are prone to act in a particular way, and explaining to your children that your partner has certain standards and routines that have to be adhered to. Time and effort will help you through.

STIM's, repeated and childish behaviours can be quite difficult to get used to, but you must understand that they are a coping mechanism. Max has lots and for most of his life has kept them in check in public, as he has learnt that often they are not considered acceptable; this has been difficult as he has constantly had to repress the urge to do them, which I suspect many other people have done. Many of these habits may become quite endearing and a source of fun and amusement for both of you. By accepting them and allowing your partner to do them in public, safe in the knowledge that you will stop them if something is not acceptable or if they are taking it a little too far, gives them great joy. They can feel relaxed and accepted. Those behaviours which are not acceptable in public or that your partner feels uncomfortable with sharing, can be saved for the safe confines of the home. By accepting that these things are an integral and necessary part of your partner's life will help both of you form a stronger relationship. Plus some of them can be extremely liberating and thoroughly good fun. Just try and relax and not worry too much about what other people think.

I find it easier to be with an Asperger husband than many might, but this is possibly because of my natural caring and patient nature. We need to do the interpreting as they find this hard. Max works at this so hard partly because when he tries, and doesn't conventionally get it right, I don't reject it; I see it as a step in the right direction. I see it from his perspective. Like the pink toilet block, he made a supreme effort to personalise it, it wasn't just an abstract thing that a woman might like he chose a pink one because I like pink!

Routines are important to Asperger's sufferers and can in some cases cause issues within a relationship, yet when we consider it we all have daily routines, getting up in time for work, going to the gym on the same days and doing the same work out. Just because our routines are slightly more flexible than those of the Asperger's sufferer shouldn't make theirs anymore unacceptable. Remember that it helps them cope with the world, they can modify the routines with time and a good reason, you just have to be patient and allow them to make the decision to change not force it on them.

Sex is something which is discussed on chat shows, on problem pages and girly magazines. We are bombarded with images and talk about sex. What is healthy, what is not, how often, where and who with, how to be successful sexually and much more. It is a source of constant discussion and open to much interpretation. The only conclusion that can be drawn is that people are overly concerned with the subject. No wonder that when things do not 'fit' with what is considered normal and healthy, questions are asked and doubts develop. There is far more to a healthy relationship than sex, I should know since in a former marriage I suffered sexual abuse and have subsequently spoken to many others who have had similar experiences. The gentleness, loyalty, care and affection that I now experience far outweigh any need for sex. We are very lucky that occasionally we have an intimate relationship, which is wonderful and exhilarating, but we do not need this for our relationship to be strong and healthy. I consider myself very lucky to have found such a wonderful man, we are soul mates.

Patience is vital and is the main thing that Max most appreciates about me. He often asks me how I put up with him. I think it is because I love him and am prepared to do whatever it takes. I am not saying it is easy because it certainly isn't, but if you want your relationship to work then this is a skill you have to refine.

I love Max's intelligence as we can talk for hours on a wide range of subjects, there are no hidden agendas as he will just say what was on his mind and not try to deceive or trick me. His lack of social boundaries makes life very exciting, and he has a great sense of humour which means we laugh all the time. One of the nicest things is that we never take each other for granted, please and thank you are so simple yet overlooked so often in relationships which are established. It is lovely to know that you are appreciated for everything you do no matter how small or routine.

Knowledge is power; the more you find out about the syndrome the easier it is to discuss things and identify ways to get round problems

The fact that you have been 'chosen' to share their life is a great honour and not one to be taken lightly. It is important to remember this, as they often find it very difficult to allow people to get close to them for fear of being rejected.

There are many aspects of having Asperger's syndrome that actually make the world a more joyous place and it is very easy to forget that. There is an honest innocence to their thinking and behaviour, that many people lose as they get older and take on the burdens of adulthood... It is wonderful to regain these simple things in such a chaotic and stressful world. Sometimes we need to question the way we view the world and ask if our way is right or the Asperger way is right. I now firmly believe that the Asperger view is often a better way, simple, innocent and fun. Having fun and enjoyment make a successful relationship, enjoy the simple things, life is too short to worry about all the problems.

Appendix

I have included this test as Max and I found it very interesting and quite helpful. It reinforced the diagnosis which he had refused to accept at university, He scored 43 and I scored 14. This can also be done online. The website is listed below.

Simon Baron-Cohen AQ Test

Take   The   AQ   Test

Psychologist Simon Baron-Cohen and his colleagues at Cambridge's Autism Research Centre have created the Autism-Spectrum Quotient, or AQ, as a measure of the extent of autistic traits in adults. In the first major trial using the test, the average score in the control group was 16.4. Eighty percent of those diagnosed with autism or a related disorder scored 32 or higher. The test is not a means for making a diagnosis, however, and many who score above 32 and even meet the diagnostic criteria for mild autism or Asperger's report no difficulty functioning in their everyday lives.

	Definitely agree	**Slightly agree**	**Slightly disagree**	**Definitely disagree**
1 I prefer to do things with others rather than on my own.	⌒	⌒	⌒	⌒
2 I prefer to do things the same way over and over again.	⌒	⌒	⌒	⌒

192

3 If I try to ⌒   ⌒   ⌒   ⌒
imagine
something, I
find it very
easy to create a
picture in my
mind.

4 I frequently ⌒   ⌒   ⌒   ⌒
get so strongly
absorbed in
one thing that I
lose sight of
other things.

5 I often notice ⌒   ⌒   ⌒   ⌒
small sounds
when others do
not.

6 I usually ⌒   ⌒   ⌒   ⌒
notice car
number plates
or similar
strings of
information.

7 Other people ⌒   ⌒   ⌒   ⌒
frequently tell
me that what
I've said is
impolite, even
though I think
it is polite.

8 When I'm ⌒   ⌒   ⌒   ⌒
reading a
story, I can
easily imagine
what the

characters might look like.

9 I am fascinated ⌐   ⌐   ⌐   ⌐
by dates.

10 In a social ⌐   ⌐   ⌐   ⌐
group, I can easily keep track of several different people's conversations.

11 I find social ⌐   ⌐   ⌐   ⌐
situations easy.

12 I tend to notice ⌐   ⌐   ⌐   ⌐
details that others do not.

13 I would rather ⌐   ⌐   ⌐   ⌐
go to a library than to a party.

14 I find making ⌐   ⌐   ⌐   ⌐
up stories easy.

15 I find myself ⌐   ⌐   ⌐   ⌐
drawn more strongly to people than to things.

16 I tend to have ⌐   ⌐   ⌐   ⌐
very strong interests, which I get upset about if I can't pursue.

194

17 I enjoy social chitchat.   ⊙   ⊙   ⊙   ⊙

18 When I talk, it isn't always easy for others to get a word in edgewise.   ⊙   ⊙   ⊙   ⊙

19 I am fascinated by numbers.   ⊙   ⊙   ⊙   ⊙

20 When I'm reading a story, I find it difficult to work out the characters' intentions.   ⊙   ⊙   ⊙   ⊙

21 I don't particularly enjoy reading fiction.   ⊙   ⊙   ⊙   ⊙

22 I find it hard to make new friends.   ⊙   ⊙   ⊙   ⊙

23 I notice patterns in things all the time.   ⊙   ⊙   ⊙   ⊙

24 I would rather go to the theatre than to a museum.   ⊙   ⊙   ⊙   ⊙

25 It does not upset me if my daily routine is disturbed.   ⊙   ⊙   ⊙   ⊙

195

26 I frequently find that I don't know how to keep a conversation going. ○ ○ ○ ○

27 I find it easy to 'read between the lines' when someone is talking to me. ○ ○ ○ ○

28 I usually concentrate more on the whole picture, rather than on the small details. ○ ○ ○ ○

29 I am not very good at remembering phone numbers. ○ ○ ○ ○

30 I don't usually notice small changes in a situation or a person's appearance. ○ ○ ○ ○

31 I know how to tell if someone listening to me is getting bored. ○ ○ ○ ○

32 I find it easy to ○ ○ ○ ○

196

do more than one thing at once.

33 When I talk on the phone, I'm not sure when it's my turn to speak. ⌒ ⌒ ⌒ ⌒

34 I enjoy doing things spontaneously. ⌒ ⌒ ⌒ ⌒

35 I am often the last to understand the point of a joke. ⌒ ⌒ ⌒ ⌒

36 I find it easy to work out what someone is thinking or feeling just by looking at their face. ⌒ ⌒ ⌒ ⌒

37 If there is an interruption, I can switch back to what I was doing very quickly. ⌒ ⌒ ⌒ ⌒

38 I am good at social chitchat. ⌒ ⌒ ⌒ ⌒

39 People often tell me that I keep going on and on about the same thing. ⌒ ⌒ ⌒ ⌒

197

40 When I was ⌒   ⌒   ⌒   ⌒
young, I used
to   enjoy
playing games
involving
pretending
with   other
children.

41 I like to collect ⌒   ⌒   ⌒   ⌒
information
about
categories of
things   (e.g.,
types of cars,
birds,   trains,
plants).

42 I   find   it ⌒   ⌒   ⌒   ⌒
difficult   to
imagine what
it would   be
like   to   be
someone else.

43 I   like   to ⌒   ⌒   ⌒   ⌒
carefully plan
any activities I
participate in.

44 I enjoy social ⌒   ⌒   ⌒   ⌒
occasions.

45 I   find   it ⌒   ⌒   ⌒   ⌒
difficult   to
work   out
people's
intentions.

46 New situations ⌒   ⌒   ⌒   ⌒
make   me

anxious.

47 I enjoy meeting new people.	⌐	⌐	⌐	⌐
48 I am a good diplomat.	⌐	⌐	⌐	⌐
49 I am not very good at remembering people's date of birth.	⌐	⌐	⌐	⌐
50 I find it very easy to play games with children that involve pretending.	⌐	⌐	⌐	⌐

How to score: "Definitely agree" or "Slightly agree" responses to questions 2, 4, 5, 6, 7, 9, 12, 13, 16, 18, 19, 20, 21, 22, 23, 26, 33, 35, 39, 41, 42, 43, 45, 46 score 1 point. "Definitely disagree" or "Slightly disagree" responses to questions 1, 3, 8, 10, 11, 14, 15, 17, 24, 25, 27, 28, 29, 30, 31, 32, 34, 36, 37, 38, 40, 44, 47, 48, 49, 50 score 1 point.

http://archive.wired.com/wired/archive/9.12/aqtest.html

copy; MRC-SBC/SJW February 1998. Published: *Journal of Autism and Developmental Disorders,* 31, 5-17 (2001).

Bibliography

Gisela & Christopher Slater-Walker (2002) 'An Asperger Marriage' London Jessica Kingsley Publishers.

Genevieve Edmonds & Luke Beardon (2008) 'Asperger Syndrome &Social Relationships': Adults Speak out about Asperger Syndrome. London Jessica Kingsley Publishers.

Maxine Ason (2003) 'Asperger's in Love': Couple Relationships and Family Affairs. London Jessica Kingsley Publishers.

Tony Attwood (1998) 'Asperger's Syndrome': A guide for parents and professionals. London Jessica Kingsley Publishers.

Sarah Hendrickx and Keith Newton (2007) Asperger |Syndrome- a love story. London Jessica Kingsley Publishers.

Rudy Simone (2009) '22 Things a woman Must Know if she loves a man with Asperger's syndrome' London Jessica Kingsley Publishers.

Dr Ruth Searle (2010)'Asperger Syndrome in Adults': A guide to realizing your potential. London. Sheldon Press.

Uta Frith (2008) 'Autism': A Very Short Introduction. New York Oxford University Press Inc.

MRC-SBC/SJW February 1998. Published: *Journal of Autism and Developmental Disorders,* 31, 5-17 (2001).

(Ehlers and Gilberg 1993; Ghaziuddin et al. 1994; Gilberg 1989; Szatmari et al. 1990; Tantum 1991)".

http://autism.wikia.com/wiki/Stimming

http://www.brighttots.com/Echolalia_Child_Autism

http://archive.wired.com/wired/archive/9.12/aqtest.html

Also published by Llanerch:

MEDICINE TREE
John Sharkey

THE ARCHERS CRAFT
Adrian Eliot Hodgkin

CORNISH DROLLS
Joseph Henry Pearce

JOSEPH OF ARIMATHIE
Rev. Walter W Skeat

DECODING ALCHEMY
Robert Anderson Plimer

THE PHYSICIANS OF MYDDFAI
John Pughe

A GUIDE TO THE SAINTS OF
WALES AND THE WEST COUNTRY
Ray Spencer

For a complete list of c. 300 titles, small-press
editions and facsimile reprints
of Llanerch Press Ltd
publications, please visit our website:
www.llanerchpress.com
or alternatively write to:
Llanerch Press Ltd, Little Court, 48 Rectory Road
Burnham-on-Sea, Somerset. TA8 2BZ